DAVID KETTERER

Frankenstein's Creation: The Book, The Monster, and Human Reality

𝓔𝓛𝓢

English Literary Studies
University of Victoria

1979

ELS Editions
Department of English
University of Victoria
Victoria, BC
Canada V8W 3W1
www.elseditions.com

Founding Editor: Samuel L. Macey

General Editor: Luke Carson

Printed by CreateSpace

English literary studies monograph series
ISSN 0829-7681 ; 16
ISBN-10 0-920604-30-7
ISBN-13 978-0-920604-30-4

CONTENTS

REPRODUCTIONS

PREFACE

Of the small proportion of people who know *Frankenstein* from having actually read the book, an infinitesimally smaller fraction will have read the book that Mary Shelley originally wrote. The 1818 edition, published by Lackington, Hughes, Harding, Mayor and Jones, based on a text which its author began writing two years earlier when she was nineteen, was superseded by a revised text published in 1831 by Henry Colburn and Richard Bentley. On the reasonable assumption that an author's final version is the authoritative one, it is the 1831 text that has been continuously reprinted. However, in 1974 the Bobbs-Merrill edition of the 1818 text was published, edited by James Rieger, with an argument for considering it the superior version. Rieger believes that Shelley's corrections and additions are more substantial than cosmetic and that therefore the 1818 text best represents the intentions of what was, in effect, a combined authorship. The question arises, should studies of *Frankenstein* take as their primary object the 1818 text rather than that of 1831?

I believe that Rieger is wrong and consequently my reading focusses primarily on the 1831 text although its basic strategy and conclusions take account of, and apply equally to, the 1818 text. Clearly, any student of *Frankenstein* who aims at being in any way comprehensive must familiarize himself with all the available textual evidence. Only by examining the manuscript fragments, which form part of the Lord Abinger collection of Shelley and Godwin materials in the Bodleian Library, comparing them with the 1818 edition, and comparing the 1818 edition with that of 1831, can Rieger's argument be tested. There is also the evidence provided by Mary's notes and corrections in a copy of the 1818 edition that she gave to Mrs. Thomas in 1823. These autograph additions, now publicly available for the first time in Rieger's edition of the 1818 text, point to some of the changes in the 1831 edition. However, when Mary made those changes she did so without being able to refer to her annotations in the copy that she gave to Mrs. Thomas.

In my opinion, a comparative study of the *Frankenstein* materials (such as that undertaken in the Appendix) upholds the established view that the 1831 edition is the preferable one. Consequently, I treat the manuscript version, the 1818 edition, and the Thomas copy marginalia as the sources of three successive sets of textual variants. This kind of comparative concern is usually only reserved for the most valued works of world literature, a class in which *Frankenstein* is not usually included. But here the established view is in need of revision. Albeit that everything else Mary Shelley wrote is at best second-rate, *Frankenstein is* a masterpiece. It is hoped that the following pages, in the course of integrating previous scholarship and building towards a new interpretation of the work, will at least help to demonstrate that fact.

ACKNOWLEDGEMENTS

My indebtedness to the scholars and critics who have contributed to our understanding of *Frankenstein* is everywhere apparent in my text. Recent listings of the wealth of commentary include W. H. Lyles, *Mary Shelley: An Annotated Bibliography* (New York: Garland Publishing, 1975), and (if I may be allowed a moment of self-acknowledgement) my own "Mary Shelley and Science Fiction: A Select Bibliography Selectively Annotated," *Science-Fiction Studies*, 5 (July 1978), 172-78. Since this study, like *Frankenstein* itself, is a somewhat composite work, I have frequent occasion to record my more specific acknowledgements in the form of footnotes.

One does not always have to agree with a scholar's findings in order to benefit from them. In this regard, special mention should be made of James Rieger whose work on *Frankenstein* (with which it should be emphasized I do not always disagree) has proved particularly stimulating. I was also prompted in a couple of fruitful directions by one of my students, Elizabeth Riehn.

The manuscript was initially drafted during the tenure of a 1976-77 Leave Fellowship from the Canada Council. Without that financial aid and the time that it bought, this study would not now exist. As in the case of a previous project, I am grateful to Robert Philmus and Darko Suvin for reading through the entire work and commenting helpfully. And once again my manuscript, expertly proofed and corrected by Wim van Voorst van Beest, was efficiently converted into its final typed state by Gene Fryer. The three pages from the manuscript fragments of *Frankenstein* are reproduced here for the first time with the kind permission of Lord Abinger.

CHAPTER ONE

"Workshop as Filthy Creation": The Book as Monster

While Henry James's description of certain novels as "loose and baggy monsters"[1] might be applied generally to his theoretical conception of the capaciousness of the novel form, the phrase has a specific and unique appropriateness as applied to Mary Shelley's *Frankenstein*. Not only is *Frankenstein* itself a very mixed narrative bag but it may also serve as a convenient illustration of how the novel came by its heterogeneous nature, that conjunction of techniques derived from the drama and the classical epic, that assimilative bagginess which James so admired. If, as Northrop Frye proposes,[2] the novel is viewed not in opposition to the romance but as a displacement, in terms of conventions of credibility, of the concerns of the romance (which are in turn the result of a more liberal conventionalized displacement of mythic archetypes), then *Frankenstein* provides a microcosmic model of these hierarchic transformations.

The subtitle, *The Modern Prometheus*, points directly to the mythic origins of Mary Shelley's plot. At the same time, within the narrative, the reader is constantly directed to make comparisons with the Christian myths of Lucifer's downfall and Adam's creation, myths related to aspects of the Prometheus story. Historically considered, the book occupies a transitional position in the tradition of the gothic romances. Many of its characteristics—the emphasis on horror and incest patterns—are paralleled in such early examples of the genre as Horace Walpole's *The Castle of Otranto* (1764), Anne Radcliffe's *The Mysteries of Udolpho* (1794) and M. G. Lewis's *The Monk* (1796). But in other respects, its psychological and epistemological probings, it points forward to the sophisticated fulfilment of *Wuthering Heights* (1874) and *Moby-Dick* (1851). *Frankenstein* is unlike the gothic romance in that the supernatural is apparently excluded as a causal factor. The pseudo-scientific explanation for the monster's existence goes beyond the "explained gothic" of such as Charles Brockden Brown and Nathaniel Hawthorne to assure the book a significant place in the evolution of that genre now known as science fiction. It is possible to regard science fiction as an amalgam of the thematic extravagancies of the romance with the realistic discipline of the novel. This

9

kind of amalgam also occurs in *Frankenstein*. Indeed, as George Levine argues, there is much in the book that relates it to the tradition of realism, in particular its moral ideals of "compromise, moderation, commitment to family and community."[3] To the degree that Frankenstein emphasizes domestic affection he is a realist hero.

Clearly, then, Mary's[4] book, as a model of novelistic heterogeneity, is a "loose and baggy monster" in the Jamesian sense. But is it also a monster in the sense that her man-made creature is a monster? Is it ill-made, ugly and horrifying? Certainly some contemporary reviewers reacted to the book as they might have done to the monster himself. The *Quarterly Review* offers a summary of the plot in order to illustrate what a "tissue of horrible and disgusting absurdity this work presents." Whether consciously or not, an image is here evoked of the physical human tissue employed in the composition of the monster. Certain merits are allowed but ultimately "Our taste and our judgement alike revolt at this kind of writing. . . . "[5] William Beckford, himself no stranger to gothic imaginings, writes on the fly-leaf of his copy of *Frankenstein*, "This is, perhaps, the foulest Toadstool that has yet sprung up from the reeking dunghill of the present times."[6] Like the monster, the book was something new under the sun, something freakish on the literary landscape. While William Godwin reacted positively to his daughter's book, he also chose to speak metaphorically of an equation between the novel and a living being: "*Frankenstein* was a fine thing: it was compressed, muscular, and firm; nothing relaxed and weak; no proud flesh."[7] He had in mind something decidedly un-loose and un-baggy.

The monster is an object of alarm not only because he is different but because he appears to be assembled imperfectly. Similarly, for all its symmetry and concentric design, there is something unsatisfactory about the book's construction. Much of the plot is absurdly contrived, melodramatic and coincidental; the language is often stilted. Somehow the whole thing does not quite hang together; it defeats consistent interpretation. Is the monster real or is he an aspect of Frankenstein? If he is an aspect of Frankenstein, what of the other characters and the environmental features of the novel? Are they real or illusory? The subjective dimension of the narrative appears to be in conflict with the monster's Lockean account of his growing understanding in terms of the impact of external influences on the *tabula rasa* of his mind. It is no wonder that the many re-creations of *Frankenstein* fail to duplicate Mary Shelley's original. For the sake of coherence different elements must be omitted. The spinoffs testify not only to the fact that *Frankenstein* does touch a mythic nerve but also to the sense that the book is seriously flawed and requires redoing. Certainly Mary Shelley herself was not content with her work as originally published and attempted to produce an improved version. But in spite of the revisions of the second edition, the basic sense of something disjunctive remains.

It has often been remarked that the popular misunderstanding that the name Frankenstein belongs to the monster and not his creator actually reveals insight into the doppelgänger relationship between the two characters. But equally, as the title of a book which is in some fashion a monstrous creation, *Frankenstein is* the name of a monster.

Of course, this fanciful analogy between the book and Frankenstein's creation may be more productive of critical illumination if it can be demonstrated that Mary Shelley herself believed she was about the business of constructing a monster. There is evidence in the text to suggest that this was the case. *Frankenstein* does seem to belong to that class of works such as William Golding's *The Spire* in which the subject matter involving a creator and his creation is metaphoric in a way that allows the author to treat the nature of his own creative process. In the 1831 Introduction Mary describes the now familiar circumstances of her story's genesis in the context of a ghost-story competition proposed by Lord Byron in mid-July, 1816, at his residence near Geneva, the Villa Diodati. Aside from Mary and Shelley (staying at the nearby Maison Chappuis, which like Diodati fronted on Lac Léman), the contestants included Byron's friend, Dr. Polidori. Mary recalls how talk of the galvanic experiments of Dr. Erasmus Darwin, a subject about which Dr. Polidori was knowledgeable, led to the vision in which a patchwork corpse was brought to life. Clearly, galvanism not only gave life to the monster but also fired the creative spark in Mary Shelley: "The idea so possessed my mind, that a thrill of fear ran through me" (p. 9) ;[8] like an electrical current, one is tempted to add.

The process of literary creation is presented in the Introduction as exactly parallel to the initial phases of the monster's apprehension of his existence: "invention, it must be humbly admitted, does not consist in creating out of a void, but out of chaos; the materials must, in the first place, be afforded: it can give form to dark, shapeless substances, but cannot bring into being the substance itself" (p. 8). Like the literary world, the monster's awareness of an outside world involves an ordering and clarifying of originally chaotic impressions. Darkness and "A strange multiplicity of sensations" (p. 102) give way to light and distinct forms. In both cases the philosophical assumption is consistent with Lockean positivism. And of both processes, the monster's own creation from afforded "materials" (pp. 54, 55) would seem to be symbolic.

In Mary's vision, "the student of unhallowed arts" is called an "artist" (p. 9) and Frankenstein speaks of himself as "an artist occupied by his favourite employment" (p. 56). Later, Frankenstein twice describes himself as the "author" (pp. 91, 101) of the evil circumstances consequent upon the monster's creation. The monster himself refers to Frankenstein as "the author at once of my existence and of its unspeakable torments" (p. 220). The writer, like the scientist, works best in isolation. In both cases, this habit of removal may impair the capacity for emotional involvement. Walton regrets the lack of a friend with whom to communicate and finds that writing is no substitute: "I shall commit my thoughts to paper, it is true; but that is a poor medium for the communication of feeling" (p. 19). Frankenstein and the writer are engaged in essentially intellectual acts.

In many respects, then, scientific and artistic creation are understood as indistinguishable. The monster values a command of language, "the science of words and letters" (p. 109), as "a godlike science" (p. 112). Franken-stein's godlike act of creation is, of course, actually the creation of Mary Shelley's language. The equation between the monster and the entire manu-script is further underscored by the passage describing Frankenstein's concern with the accuracy of Walton's notes: "he asked to see them, and then himself corrected and augmented them in many places; but principally in *giving the life and spirit* to the conversations he held with his enemy. 'Since you have *preserved* my narration,' said he, 'I would not that a *mutilated* one should go down to posterity,' " (p. 210; my italics). The words italicized strongly sug-gest an analogy with the botched monster.

Towards the conclusion of the book, the monster twice refers to his life rather oddly as the "series of my being" (pp. 219, 222). Mary seems to have deliberately insinuated these two references during the typesetting process. They are conspicuously absent from the manuscript version. Clearly, at a retrospective stage, she attached a particular importance to the repetition of the same phrase. In part, the phrase conveys the idea that, as something in process, the monster cannot be neatly categorized and understood. But I believe that Mary had an additional intention which is relevant to the present context. On other occasions, she uses the word "series" in a specifically bookish sense. Her Introduction opens with a reference to Colburn and Bentley, "The Publishers of the Standard Novels, selecting *Frankenstein* for one of their series...." *Frankenstein* was, in fact, originally published as a series of three volumes. Mary goes on to describe how, as a child, she would "write stories" by "following up trains of thought, which had for their sub-ject the formation of a succession of imaginary incidents" (p. 5). The details of a story might be said to constitute a series and that is indeed how Walton describes his narrative to his sister: "my tale conveys in its series internal evidence of the events of which it is composed" (p. 30). Another document, the journal that the monster finds in the pocket of the garment he took from the laboratory, details that "series of disgusting circumstances" leading to his "accursed origin" (p. 130). It seems likely, therefore, that the idiosyncratic phrase "series of my being" is in part intended to relate the monster's individual history to the succession of incidents that make up the entire narrative.

But the analogy between Mary's book and Frankensein's creation is perhaps most strikingly pointed up by the way in which the animation of the monster is dramatized. The cinematic iconography of an inert form stretched out on a slab, then slowly sitting up after being electrically jolted into life amidst an assemblage of retorts and scientific apparatus, barely exists in Mary's narrative. Rather, in terms of imaginative impact, the monster appears to emerge from Frankenstein's dream much as the monster and the idea for the book first came to Mary in a vision (she was in bed but could not, she claims, sleep). Frankenstein awakens from a dream in which he is embracing his dead mother to find his creature standing by his bedside. It is actually Mary's vision as described in the Introduction which provides the clearest basis for the epiphanic film image: "I saw the hideous phantasm of a man stretched out, and then, on the working of some powerful engine, show signs of life and stir with an uneasy, half-vital motion." As in the narrative itself, Frankenstein rushes from his handiwork: "He sleeps; but he is awakened; he opens his eyes; behold the horrid thing stands at his bedside . . ." (p. 9). The next day Mary began with the words (which appear on the manuscript sheet reproduced following this page) that begin Chapter 5 in the revised edition (and that now seem anticipative of the opening of a Snoopy novel) : "It was on a dreary night of November . . ." (p. 57). She skimps the factual details of the monster's animation and builds up the situation after Frankenstein has taken to his bed. Essentially, Mary here follows the substance of her vision except that considerable emphasis is now given to the fact that Frankenstein himself, while sleeping, experiences a visionary dream which leads to the presence of the monster. Clearly, we are to understand that the novel and the monster are both in a sense dream creations.

If it be accepted that Mary saw Frankenstein's activity in his "workshop of filthy creation" (p. 55) as directly analogous to her own, perhaps the process of the one may be usefully applied to the process of the other. Broadly speaking, the creation of the monster takes place in three stages. First, Frankenstein has the task of collecting what Mary's Introduction terms "the component parts" (p. 9), the various limbs and organs that go to make a human being. Second comes the matter of assembly and arrange-

It was on a dreary night of November
that I beheld ~~the frame on which~~ my man compleated, and
with an anxiety that almost amount
ed to agony, I collected ~~the~~ instruments of life
around me ~~and endeavoured~~ ~~that I might~~ to infuse a
spark of being into the lifeless thing
that lay at my feet. It was already
one in the morning, the rain pattered
dismally against the window panes &
my candle was nearly burnt out, when
by the glimmer of the half extinguish
ed light I saw the dull yellow eye of
the creature open — It breathed hard,
and a convulsive motion agitated
its limbs.

~~But how~~ How can I describe my
emotion at this catastrophe, or how deli
neate the wretch whom with such in
infinite pains and care I had endeavoured
to form. His limbs were in proportion
beautiful. and I had selected his features & as
~~handsome~~ ~~handsome~~ ~~Handsome~~ beautiful Great God! his
yellow ~~dun~~ skin scarcely covered the work of
of a lustrous black & muscles and arteries beneath; his hair
was flowing and his teeth of a pearly white
ness but ~~these~~ luxuriances only ~~formed~~.
formed a more horrid contrast with
his watery eyes that seemed almost of
the same colour as the dun white
sockets in which they were set,

ment according to the principles of human anatomy. Third and of most importance is the creative galvanic spark which gives life to the inert form.

These three stages readily correspond to the different aspects of the narrative treated in the three chapters following. If the monster is made of bits of other men, the book itself is very much a patchwork of bits and pieces from other books. In fact, as Chapter 2 attempts to demonstrate, an understanding of *Frankenstein* calls for some knowledge of all manner of extrinsic materials, literary, philosophical, biographical, psychological, social and historical. To invoke the "biographical fallacy" and banish this material is to render much of *Frankenstein* inoperative or pointless. The book unquestionably gains in meaning if a reader brings to it some knowledge of Mary's literary sources—the tradition of the gothic novel, the epistolary novel, Godwin's novels, *Paradise Lost*, "The Ancient Mariner," and Shelley's poetry—to mention the most obvious examples—and some knowledge of Mary's circumstances. There is no doubt that her psychological preoccupations, her relationships and the times in which she lived have left a profound imprint on the book. Given the disparate elements that went into the work, Mary might well say with Frankenstein, "having spent some months in successfully collecting and arranging my materials, I began" (p. 54).

Necessarily, the arrangement of Mary's materials proceeded according to certain thematic determinations just as Frankenstein arranged his bits and pieces according to the design of a man. The thematic aspects of *Frankenstein*, the subject of Chapter 3, are evident on the basis of intrinsic connections. Many details cohere in such a way as to suggest that some kind of dialectic between an alienating egotism and warm human relationships is of thematic importance. Other details point to the development of a doppelgänger theme, the growing sense that the monster is a projection of Frankenstein's psyche. The externalizing emphasis of the first theme and the internalized emphasis of the second make for troubling contradictions on any logical level.

Within the context of the novel, the logical problems are resolved by the kind of metaphorical transcendence that, it may be ventured, defines a work of art. The monster as a metaphorical aspect of Frankenstein, as a metaphor for the entire narrative world, and indeed, as will become increasingly apparent, as a metaphor for reality itself embodies this transcendent reconciliation. Something of this reconciliation is also implied by the relationship, which Marc A. Rubenstein has drawn attention to, between the structural pole at the centre of the concentric narrative rings and Walton's polar destination.[9] But the structurally central element of the narrative, the story of Safie's independent mother, is not, as Rubenstein would have it, the exact equivalent in import of the North Pole. One pole is internal and of seemingly psychological import, the other is external and of something like mythological import. The likelihood that the psychological and the mythological are congruent is implied but not confirmed. At the same time, of supreme importance to the novel's metaphoric vitality, and the subject of Chapter 4, is the use Mary makes of the natural sublime and magnetism as tokens of transcendence. All these features correspond, of course, to the third and final stage whereby Frankenstein's creation is imbued with life.

Much that is cryptic and hazy in the above outline (a scheme, incidentally, that has the additional advantage of enabling me to draw synthetically upon, and assimilate most of, the valuable if contradictory scholarship that has grown up around *Frankenstein* over the last few years) will be filled out and clarified in the pages that follow. However, one aspect of my pluralistic, three-stage approach should be considered here. The relationship between external elements, internal elements and bridging metaphoric elements might be loosely equated with the book's concentric structure: Walton's outer narrative ring, the monster's inner core and Frankenstein's intermediate ring.

But Mary seems to have worked to blur any such clear structural distinctions. The outer ring is concerned with the exploration of the realities of an external world but that reality is of an increasingly surrealistic nature. Correspondingly, the inner core, which one might expect to be predominantly subjective, presents in its description of the monster's education the most positivistically informed, outer-directed aspect of the book. Structurally, then, the book reflects the basic problem that the monster poses: what is his nature; is he an aspect of Frankenstein or does he have a genuine independent existence? One might illustrate the conundrum further by noting that the *tabula rasa* which is the initial state of the monster's mind is made objectively manifest by the polar landscape.

The internal/external "contradiction" and the relationships I have set up between extrinsic elements and intrinsic thematic structures imply, of course, that the novel is concerned with that basic philosophical crux, the subjectivity or objectivity of reality. However, the case for, and the radical interpretive implications of, this possibility must await my concluding chapter.

CHAPTER TWO

"Component Parts":
Extrinsic Materials

There is no clear relationship between the extent to which a work can be shown to be variously derivative and the question of its originality. *Frankenstein* is both extraordinarily original and extraordinarily derivative. This is not as paradoxical as it may sound since what is thought to be creative or original about any human production is essentially a matter of perceiving unexplored possibilities of arrangement and relationship and therefore, strictly speaking, is not creative or original at all. The notion in Mary's 1831 Introduction, taken probably from either Locke or Hume, that "Invention . . . does not consist in creating out of a void, . . . the materials must, in the first place be afforded" (p. 8), applies, as we have seen, equally to her book and to Frankenstein's synthetic being.

In the case of Mary's "materials," the "component parts" (p. 9) of her creation, source hunters have faced few problems of identification. Mary kept an almost daily record of her reading—in addition to compiling yearly lists of books read—in the *Journal* that she and Shelley began jointly on July 28, 1814. The basic work of checking the entries and lists for the period up to and including 1816 has clearly revealed which texts, in addition to those directly alluded to in *Frankenstein*, were most germane to the composition of that masterpiece. Much of the material that went into *Frankenstein* Mary derived not from other books but from her own experience and knowledge of the world around her. Again most of the evidence is readily available. Our detailed knowledge of many of the people with whom she was associated has enabled critics to speculate with some assurance concerning the biographical and psychological factors in *Frankenstein*. Associated by birth with the Godwin circle and by marriage with Shelley's circle, Mary was uniquely placed in relation to the entire development of English Romanticism. Consequently, many of the influences and obsessions which make up what we understand as the Romantic movement are reflected microscopically in *Frankenstein*. Indeed, *Frankenstein* might be said to present Romanticism in a nutshell.[1]

Since any creative work can be located in relation to a network of influences and personal experiences, it may be suspected that *Frankenstein* appears to be more a work of compilation than it actually is simply because we are relatively well informed about the contributing circumstances. However, it does seem likely that Mary was unusually conscious of the extent to which, in "creating" *Frankenstein*, she was actually involved in the business of compiling and arranging an assortment of diverse materials. At the age of nineteen she must have been aware of the need to go beyond her own experiences in the search for inspiration. In covering this ground, my own activity will be largely derivative although, in pulling together and arranging materials gone over by other critics, I hope to provide a fuller synthesis than has previously been attempted. With one or two exceptions, what is original in the following survey is confined to the consideration of what interpretive weight should be attached to the various sources and influences.

The materials with which I am here concerned are "extrinsic" in the sense that their elucidation requires a certain specialized knowledge which is not adequately provided by the text of *Frankenstein* itself. There are other aspects of *Frankenstein*—primarily, the doppelgänger theme, the use made of magnetism and electricity, the book's philosophical dimension—where it is relevant or possible to speak of external influences. But these aspects are so much a part of the overall design of *Frankenstein* that any external elucidative context is only of secondary importance. I am presently concerned with those localized features of the text where an external elucidative context is of primary importance. The other *secondarily* extrinsic elements will receive detailed attention in succeeding chapters in the context of what is thematically and imagistically intrinsic to *Frankenstein*.

This distillation of the intrinsic and the extrinsic is obviously a tricky business and, as will become increasingly apparent, the ambiguity of internality and externality is central to the meaning of *Frankenstein*. Likewise, the distinction implied by the two sections following, the one devoted to literary and the other to non-literary sources, is more approximate than absolute. The problem becomes particularly acute in considering Shelley's influence. How can one distinguish in *Frankenstein* between the influence of Shelley the man and the influence of Shelley's poetry? At the same time, it should be appreciated that the non-literary sources were both internal or psychological and external or social and historical. The two sections in this chapter and in Chapters 3 and 4 fracture elements which may ultimately be seen as unified. In this respect, my strategy reflects Mary Shelley's.

(i) *Embodied Texts*

All literary movements involve a selective reinterpretation and assimilation of previous forms and themes. To a marked extent, the elements that might be said to be redrawn by Romanticism are also redrawn by *Frankenstein*. Hence its representative character. Many of these elements may be understood as loosely related manifestations of the Prometheus myth, first, in pagan or classical literature, second, as revised in Christian terms, allowing, most spectacularly, for some of the ambiguities in *Paradise Lost*,[2] and third, amongst the literary consequences of what may be regarded as its application and the resultant growth of scientific knowledge during the period known as the Enlightenment. The Romantic movement is often defined in terms of its largely rebellious relationship to the Enlightenment. It is the quality of Promethean rebelliousness that causes a writer such as Blake or Shelley, in reinterpreting *Paradise Lost*, to side with Satan.

But the influence of the Promethean archetype is nowhere more apparent than in the work produced by Mary, Shelley and Byron during and following the Geneva summer of 1816. Byron wrote the poem "Prometheus" in July, 1816, and in September began his dramatic account of the Promethean exploits of the eponymous Manfred. Between 1818 and 1819 Shelley, inspired by the *Prometheus Bound* of Aeschylus, wrote his version of the missing conclusion, *Prometheus Unbound*. Mary announces her indebtedness by the subtitle identification of Frankenstein as *The Modern Prometheus*.

While most versions of the Prometheus myth are concerned only with *Prometheus pyrphoros*, the Greek god who revolted against Zeus, stole fire from heaven and gave it to man, in *Frankenstein* the figure of *Prometheus plasticator*, the creator of man, is more immediately relevant. *Prometheus plasticator* may or may not have been part of the original myth but, as described in a number of Roman versions, he shapes man out of clay. Mary would have come across one such version while struggling, with Shelley's help, through the original text of Ovid's *Metamorphoses* from April 8 to May 13, 1815.[3] Dryden translates the relevant passage as follows:

> Whether with particles of Heav'nly fire
> The God of Nature did his Soul inspire,
> Or Earth, but new divided from the Skie,
> And, pliant, still, retain'd the Aethereal Energy:
> Which Wise *Prometheus* temper'd into paste,
> And mix't with living Streams, the Godlike Image caste . . .
> From such rude Principles our Form began;
> And Earth was Metamorphos'd into Man.[4]

19

As adapted to early Christian belief, Prometheus animates with the flame of life the figure originally moulded by God. The reversion to the rebellious *Prometheus pyrphoros* and his equation with Satan is a later development.

There is no evidence of Prometheus playing a part in the animation of a female figure[5] but later in the *Metamorphoses* Mary may have read the account of the animation (by Aphrodite) of the female figure which Pygmalion sculpted and with which he fell in love. If Mary did not read this story in Ovid, she certainly read it in *Nouveaux Contes Moraux et Nouvelles Historiques* (1802). One of the playlets in this collection is entitled *Pygmalion et Galatéa; ou La Statue animée depuis vingt-quatre heures.* Mary's *Journal* entry for July 24, 1816, links this collection (albeit inaccurately entitled) with the composition of *Frankenstein*: "I read Madame de Genlis's 'Nouvelles Nouvelles,' and write my story." She records completing the collection on August 23rd.[6] Furthermore, Burton D. Pollin suggests that the awakening of the innocent Galatéa and her gradual awareness of the evils of society provided hints for the process whereby the monster becomes educated in the ways of the world.[7]

Mary may have had some familiarity with other legends involving the animation of inert figures; for example, stories associated with the Golem, a huge clay statue periodically animated by a rabbi supposedly in the cause of Jewish vengeance. In some versions of the legend, the golem, like Frankenstein's monster, turns on his master. Certainly, the stories of medieval alchemists creating homunculi must be counted as of some relevance to the creation of Mary's book. Such projects would have formed the basis of Frankenstein's early obsession with alchemy.

In this connection and with the aid of the manuscript version of *Frankenstein*, I wish to introduce a likely "source" that has hitherto been overlooked. Before proceeding to the Orkneys alone, Frankenstein travels with Clerval northwards through England, stopping at places of interest. According to the manuscript version as reproduced following this page, while in Oxford touring the university, Frankenstein is reminded of a former resident, "Chancellor" Bacon and his experiments with gunpowder. Alongside this passage occurs Shelley's most personal annotation: "No sweet Pecksie[8]—'twas *frier* Bacon—the discoverer of gunpowder." Her confusion aside, clearly Mary was aware that someone of scientific bent named Bacon was associated with Oxford. The most likely source for her knowledge of the man would have been Robert Greene's play, *The Honourable History of Friar Bacon, and Frier Bougay* (written about 1589, published in 1594), which derived in part from a mid-sixteenth-century work entitled *The Famous Historie of Fryer Bacon.*

20

112

with curiosity the models instituted by the author
of the history ... there also shewn a room
which ... had ... Hamilton Buttry
as it was predicted
would fall in when a man ...
that philosopher should enter it ...
or who accompanied me refused to pass
the threshold, although we ventured inside
in perfect safety security

Matlock, which was our next
place of rest, resembled to a great degree
the scenery of Switzerland. But everything
is on a lower scale & the green mountains
want the crown of distant white alps
which always attend on the pine ...
mountains of our country. We visited
the wondrous cave & the little cabinets
of natural history where the curiosities
are disposed in the same manner
as in the collections at Servoz & Chamou-
nix. The latter name made me tremble
when pronounced by Henry & I hastened
to quit Matlock where the scenes were
thus associated

From Derby, still journeying northward, we passed two months among the
mountains of Cumberland & Westmorland.
I could now almost fancy myself among
the Swiss mountains. The little patches of
snow which yet lingered on the northern
sides of the mountains - the lakes & the
dashing of the rocky mountain streams
were all to me familiar & dear sights
to me. Here also we made some acquain-

From the *Historie* Greene took one of his central ingredients: the mechanical talking head. In the play an Oxford doctor tells Frier Bacon of reports he has heard that

> Th'art making of a brazen head by art
> Which shall unfold strange doubts and aphorisms
> And read a lecture in philosophy. . . .[9]

It should be noted that Albertus Magnus, one of Frankenstein's admired alchemists, supposedly made a complete man out of brass to do the housework and, like Bacon's brass head, answer philosophical questions. There is, in fact, a literary tradition of mechanical men, the most famous being Sir Arthegall's iron-man Talus in Spenser's *Faerie Queene*. True, Bacon only makes an animated head but he still qualifies as a shadowy protoype of Frankenstein. Moreover, what is accomplished in the play by alchemy and black magic comes about through scientific research in the *Historie*. The man himself, Roger Bacon, who lived from around 1220 to 1294, was known as *doctor mirabilis* and, like Frankenstein, had an unquenchable thirst for knowledge. Amongst his many and varied activities, he completed a three-volume encyclopedia of all the known sciences. In revising her manuscript, rather than change "Chancellor" Bacon to Friar Bacon, Mary decided to omit the entire episode. Perhaps she did so because the parallels set up between Roger Bacon, Frankenstein and Shelley (who was also at Oxford for a while) were too revealing or, at least, distracting.

There is not much of the Promethean over-reacher in Greene's play but the archetype is clearly present in a related work, Marlowe's *Dr. Faustus*. Something of Marlowe's Faustus seems to have contributed to the conception of Frankenstein. The young Frankenstein, obsessed by such ancient alchemists as Agrippa, Paracelsus and Albertus Magnus, appears to be treading in Faustus's footsteps. And the ambiguity of Frankenstein's simultaneous repentance and defiance at the end is remarkably similar to the situation of Faustus, "noble and godlike in ruin!" (p. 210). Faustus's final lines before being dragged down to hell contain in equal part the accents of horror and desire:

> My God, my God! Look not so fierce on me!
> Adders and serpents, let me breathe awhile!
> Ugly hell, gape not! come not, Lucifer;
> I'll burn my books! —Ah, Mephistophilis![10]

More genuinely contrite, Green's Friar Bacon, like Shakespeare's Prospero, does abjure magic when he breaks his prospective glass. Both here and elsewhere, in fact, the interactions between *Friar Bacon and Friar Bungay*, *Dr. Faustus* and *The Tempest* make their presence felt in *Frankenstein*.

22

Frankenstein appears at his most defiant when urging Walton's crew to continue their voyage of discovery: "Do not return to your families with the stigma of disgrace marked on your brows. Return, as heroes who have fought and conquered, and who know not what it is to turn their backs on the foe" (p. 215). Here Frankenstein is echoing the words of another intellectual over-reacher, Dante's Ulysses, exhorting his sailors to continue voyaging: "Do not deny yourselves the sun, of the unpeopled world. Consider your origin: you were not formed to live like beasts, but to pursue power and knowledge."[11] By suggesting this analogy, Mary puts Frankenstein's Promethean defiance in an ironic context. Ulysses' voyage proves fatal and for talking his mariners into it, Ulysses finds himself among the evil counsellors of the *Inferno* whose souls are each enveloped in a flame. For Frankenstein, however, in the 1818 edition, "The promise of a mate I had made to the daemon weighed upon my mind, like Dante's iron cowl on the heads of the hellish hypocrites."[12] Elsewhere, incidentally, Mary must be thinking of the *Inferno* when she observes that the animated monster "became a thing such as even Dante could not have conceived" (p. 58). Here Mary herself is the over-reacher.

A kind of indirection similar to that employed in echoing Ulysses' speech attends Mary's use of one of her most important sources, *Paradise Lost*. The evidence of her indebtedness is directly there in the text and in the Preface that Shelley wrote for the 1818 edition. After mentioning "The Iliad, the tragic poetry of Greece, Shakespeare in the Tempest and Midsummer Night's Dream," Shelley singles out *Paradise Lost* as being akin to *Frankenstein* in newly combining "the elementary principles of human nature" (p. 13). But the similarity is as much a matter of content as technique. Indeed, the Christian content of *Paradise Lost* might well have suggested the Prometheus analogy: they are both myths of creation and rebellion. By association at least, Mary might almost have felt herself in Milton's presence while writing *Frankenstein* nearby the Villa Diodati. The villa, built in 1710, was owned by a descendant of Charles Diodati, a friend and former schoolfellow of Milton. In 1639, when Milton visited Geneva, he stayed not, of course, at the non-existent Villa Diodati, but he did stay at the Geneva residence of Charles' uncle, the theologian John Diodati.[13] Mary was thoroughly familiar with *Paradise Lost*. Both she and Shelley read it in 1815 and again in 1816 when, during a week in November, Mary listened to Shelley read the entire poem out loud to her almost as an accompaniment to the routine of writing *Frankenstein* which had by then established itself.[14]

It is not surprising, then, that of the bits and pieces that make up *Frankenstein*, *Paradise Lost* appears to be the most sizable. The quotation from Book X, lines 743-45, that Mary used as an epigraph to the first edition of *Franken-*

stein establishes a sense of the monster as analogous to Adam and of Franken-stein as analogous to God:

> Did I request thee, Maker, from my clay
> To mould me Man, did I solicit thee
> From darkness to promote me?

Conveniently provided with a copy of Milton's epic, the monster himself sees the Adamic parallel but discovers also that the situation of Satan, the outcast, more closely resembles his own. Spying on the De Laceys and Agatha, he is equivalent to the envious Satan surveying life in Eden. As a result the monster sees no alternative but to follow Satan's example and revolt. In justifying himself to Walton, the monster, who has been increasingly referred to as a "fiend" or "devil," echoes Satan's defiant cry at line 110 of Book IV, "Evil, be thou my good" with "Evil thenceforth became my good" (p. 220).

But these parallels serve not so much to establish *Frankenstein* as an allegorical parody of *Paradise Lost* as to augment an internal parallel between the monster and his maker. Frankenstein also likens himself to Adam, a fallen Adam barred from the "paradisiacal dreams of love and joy" (p. 189) held out to him by Elizabeth. Barred from the De Lacey "paradise," the monster describes his situation in a way that recalls the predicament of Adam (and Eve) on being forced to leave Eden: "And now, with the world before me, whither should I bend my steps?" (p. 139). Similarly for Adam and Eve, "The world was all before them . . . "[15] At the same time, Frankenstein might be viewed with his monster as akin to Satan, a rebellious over-reacher who would become the equal of his Creator. Frankenstein's "I was cursed by some devil, and carried about with me my eternal hell" (p. 203) echoes the monster's "I, like the arch fiend, bore a hell with me" (p. 136), and both recall Satan's "Which way I fly is Hell; myself am Hell . . . " and "the hot hell that always in him burns."[16]

A number of critics, including Martin Tropp,[17] have attempted to read *Frankenstein* in terms of *Paradise Lost* without taking into account the fact that Mary's reading of Milton's poem is no more orthodox than Blake's or Shelley's. The Miltonic elements do not serve as any strict kind of moral yardstick. Their function is highly ambiguous. It is implied that the roles of Adam, Satan and God are interchangeable. Consequently, we may infer both that God is Satan and that Adam or man is all.[18]

Prometheus presents man with the essential but dangerous fire of knowledge; Satan promises knowledge in the deceptively safe shape of an apple. During the period which is characterized as the Age of Enlightenment it seemed that knowledge about the nature of man and reality was becoming available as never before. Alongside and sometimes in conflict with the Christian certainties celebrated in *Paradise Lost* were arising new structures of scientific certainty. One literary consequence of this new sense of assurance was the development of realism. Mary first read Richardson's epistolary novels in 1816[19] and undoubtedly they played a part in her decision to heighten the realism of her story by presenting it in documentary form. Although, as I have indicated in Chapter 1, the realistic elements in *Frankenstein* have recently been treated by George Levine, it was Sir Walter Scott who first drew attention to the realistic style of "plain forcible English"[20] which Mary uses to domesticate her marvellous tale. Here, of course, *Robinson Crusoe* or *Gulliver's Travels* might have provided instructive models.

There is also considerable evidence in *Frankenstein* of the scientific and philosophical thought that underpins the realistic attitude. It is likely, as Brian Aldiss argues,[21] that early intimations of Darwin's theory of evolution prompted Mary to a secular conception of Genesis and to the possibility of a human *Prometheus plasticator* or a human god. Both the Shelleys knew something of the work of Dr. Erasmus Darwin (1731-1802), the botanist poet and grandfather of Charles Darwin. It is this Dr. Darwin that Mary refers to in her 1831 Introduction and that Shelley refers to in his 1818 Preface. In her account of the genesis of *Frankenstein*, Mary recalls listening to Byron and Shelley talking about "the principle of life" and "the experiments of Dr. Darwin" (p. 8). Shelley begins his Preface by observing that "The event on which this fiction is founded has been supposed, by Dr. Darwin and some of the physiological writers of Germany, as not of impossible occurrence" (p. 13). In *Zoonomia*, a two volume work published in 1794 and 1796, Darwin propounded an early view of evolution as a process of spontaneous generation and natural selection. If Mary did not read this work herself she might have found out about it from Shelley who first became acquainted with Darwin in 1811 and admired his speculative and poetical way with science, particularly in his long poem *The Botanic Garden* (1792).[22]

The experiment of Dr. Darwin, that Mary recalls as described by Shelley and Byron, seems to have had to do with galvanic electricity. I shall have something to say about Mary's imagistic use of electricity in Chapter 4, but for the moment it is sufficient to observe that the monster is animated by an electrical process and that it is surely not accidental that, while *Frankenstein* was being written in October, 1816, the Shelleys read "Davy's 'Chemistry,'" presumably his *Elements of Chemcial Philosophy* (1812).[23]

Enlightenment philosophers were much concerned with the nature of knowledge generally (including the knowledge of good and evil) and how one comes by it. In describing the monster's education, Mary makes paricular use of the psychological sensationalism of John Locke. She seems to have made a particularly intense study of his *Essay Concerning Human Understanding* beginning on November 16, 1816, continuing almost daily through December, and concluding on January 8, 1817.[24] In my final chapter, I shall have occasion to consider in some detail the extent to which *Frankenstein* reflects Locke's philosophical position, his denial of innate "ideas" and his attribution of all knowledge to sensation primarily and to reflection secondarily. Locke's philosophy led other thinkers to consider the mechanics of purely aesthetic responses. One such response is explored by Edmund Burke in his *Inquiry into the Origins of Our Ideas of the Sublime and the Beautiful* (1756). As will appear in Chapter 4, Mary's extensive treatment of sublime phenomena in *Frankenstein* reflects Burke's theory.

Another English philosopher in the Lockean tradition may have had a very specific influence on *Frankenstein*. According to M. K. Joseph, the 3rd Earl of Shaftesbury, who had once been a pupil of Locke's, may have provided an additional source for Mary's knowledge of Prometheus in his creative role. In Shaftesbury's *The Moralists*, which was published in 1709 but which we have no record of Mary's reading until 1825,[25] there are several references to *Prometheus plasticator* and the occurrence of the phrase "our modern Prometheus" (applied denigratingly to artists) may have suggested Mary's subtitle. Furthermore, in view of the relationship, for which I have argued, between the creation of the book and the creation of the monster, it is interesting to note that, in his *Advice to an Author* (1710), Shaftesbury describes the true poet as "a second maker, a just Prometheus after Jove."[26]

While the influence of Shaftesbury is conjectural, less questionable is the case for Mary's knowledge of the French philosophers who variously developed Locke's position. Condillac (the literary creator of another animated statue) demonstrates the relationship between even the most abstract of human ideas and the evidence provided by the sensations in his *Treatise on Sensations* (1754). His work was well known in England and, according to Burton R. Pollin, "likely to be cited in the Diodati discussions."[27] The work of Diderot is also of relevance here and presumably in some way familiar to Mary. She read Diderot's *La Père de Famille* (1758) in 1816 and it is possible, as Pollin suggests, that his account of the importance of sight in the development of consciousness in *Lettre sur les aveugles* (1749) may have inspired the episode in which the monster, seeking fellowship, first approaches the blind De Lacey.[28] A less likely but conceivably related source is an encyclopedic work published irregularly between 1749 and 1804, Buffon's *Histoire Naturelle*, with its presentation of a man suddenly equipped with senses. Although Mary has Frankenstein read Buffon in the 1818 text there is no evidence of her reading him until June and July, 1817, when her book had been written.[29] Perhaps she knew of the *Histoire Naturelle* from Shelley who had translated a portion of it in 1811.[30]

Locke's materialistic stance is taken to its logical limits in *L'Homme-machine* (1747-48) by Julian Offray de la Mettrie who accounts for all human thought in strictly mechanical terms. There is no evidence that Mary was familiar with this book but its title and subject matter, which point clearly in the direction of robots and intelligent computors, make it at least an interesting analogue to *Frankenstein*. Indeed, as Mario Praz observes, La Mettrie calls for "un nouveau Prométhée" to create an artificial man.[31] To what extent did Mary write *Frankenstein* in response?

Jean-Jacques Rousseau and Mary's father, William Godwin, developed the moral implications of Locke's ideas. It would, in fact, have been surprising had Rousseau not influenced *Frankenstein* since Geneva was his birthplace and the Shelley party would have seen his statue at Plainpalais. Both Mary and Shelley read Rousseau's *La Nouvelle Héloïse* (1761). While he read it in 1816, she read it several times between 1815 and 1817.[32] And it may be, as Pollin ventures, that Mary named Safie after the Sophie of Rousseau's *Emile* (1762).[33] But Rousseau is primarily associated with the concept of the Noble Savage (although the term itself is not his) and, as Milton Millhauser was the first to point out, the monster is initially presented in this role.[34] It was Rousseau who secularized the idea of an unfallen state of innocence such as that apparently enjoyed by the monster before his awareness has expanded to include some knowledge of the evil ways of society.

Given the immense importance of the environment and external stimuli, Godwin set out in his *Enquiry Concerning Political Justice and its Influence on Morals and Happiness* (1793) to describe the kind of social circumstances that would assure the maintenance of man's natural goodness. Mary dedicated her book "To William Godwin, Author of *Political Justice, Caleb Williams*, etc," by way of acknowledging his influence. But although Mary read *Political Justice* carefully in 1814[35] and although many of its ideas make their way into her text, Shelley severely distorts *Frankenstein* in his Preface when he reduces its intent to a Godwinian formula, "the exhibition of the amiableness of domestic affection, and the excellence of universal virtue" (p. 14).

Certainly the monster attributes his behaviour to Frankenstein's failure to treat him with the affection and benevolence that Godwin's sense of justice requires: "I was benevolent and good; misery made me a fiend. Make me happy, and I shall again be virtuous" (p. 100). "My vices are the children of a forced solitude that I abhor; and my virtues will necessarily arise when

27

I live in communion with an equal" (p. 147). Repeatedly he asks for "justice" in the Godwinian sense; he requires that Frankenstein fulfil his social obligation towards him. But as we shall see, the monster's evil actions cannot be explained so easily. Indeed, Christopher Small correctly observes that if *Frankenstein* is to be understood as Shelley apparently understood it in his unpublished review—"Treat a person ill and he will become wicked"—why should the demonstration of this moral entail the invention of a monster?[36] And, in the interests of consistency, it must be asked why does Frankenstein, who has had the benefits of what appears to be an affectionate and just Godwinian upbringing, feel himself to be responsible for evil and why does he come to such a sticky end?

Mary was deeply attached to her father but she was not indoctrinated by his theories. Wherever Mary appears to be adopting one of her father's ideas the overall context tends to subvert that idea. For example, Small argues that Elizabeth's adoption illustrates Godwin's view that in many cases the upbringing of a child might be more effectively undertaken by strangers than by the parents.[37] But Mary's overall purpose is to contrive a situation in which Frankenstein's love for Elizabeth has the incestuous overtones of a brother/sister relationship.

The Romantic movement both drew on and reacted to the teachings of the Enlightenment. In the person of Godwin the Enlightenment background and the Romantic reaction come together. He wrote a number of novels which derive their ideational content from his theoretical work. These melodramatic works may be loosely related in terms of their philosophical and psychological dimensions to that sub-genre of Romanticism, the gothic novel, a genre which *Frankenstein* simultaneously imitated and transformed. In fact, it is the spirit of her father's novels, particularly *Caleb Williams*, rather than of *Political Justice* which is most faithfully reproduced in *Frankenstein*.

Things as They are; or The Adventures of Caleb Williams (1794), from which Mary heard Shelley read in 1814 and which she read twice herself, once in 1814 and again in 1816,[38] develops, like *Frankenstein*, into an ambiguous tale of pursuit. The insatiably curious secretary, Caleb (like Frankenstein in his search for knowledge), discovers documents which prove his master, Falkland, to be a murderer. Having caught him in this act of discovery, Falkland swears Caleb to silence and then arranges his conviction on a fabricated charge. But Caleb escapes from prison (where, like Mary's monster, he felt himself to be at odds with society at large) only to be relentlessly pursued by Falkland who, like Frankenstein's monster, becomes increasingly fiendish. There is a final confrontation which Shelley recalls in the review of *Frankenstein* that he drafted: "The encounter and argument between Frankenstein and the Being on the sea of ice almost approaches in effect the expostulation of Caleb Williams with Falkland. It reminds us indeed somewhat of the style and character of that admirable writer to whom the author dedicated his work, and whose productions he seems to have studied [Shelley is, of course, abetting the view that *Frankenstein*, originally published anonymously, was written by a man]."[39] The similarity between the two novels, which Shelley was the first to observe, might be extended. In both cases, there is a strong sense of a symbiotic relationship between pursuer and pursued and that innocence and guilt have changed places. After Falkland has confessed and died, Caleb feels himself to be a murderer.

Something of Godwin's second novel, *St. Leon* (1799), is also imprinted on *Frankenstein*.[40] St. Leon, a man of Faustian ambitions, strikes a bargain with the Wandering Jew. He will assume the curse of immortality in exchange for the Philosopher's Stone and the Elixir of Life. Predictably, St. Leon discovers that he has doomed himself to a life of endless solitude. As Sir Walter Scott observed in his review, "*Frankenstein* is a novel upon the same plan with *St. Leon*."[41] It is also likely that the emphasis on companionship in Godwin's third novel, *Fleetwood* (1805), reinforced the ideas Mary would already have gleaned from *Political Justice*.[42]

Godwin's influence is also to be detected in the work of the American gothic novelist, Charles Brockden Brown (indeed, *Caleb Williams* was the standard to which he aspired), and, in turn, his work appears to be amongst the sources of *Frankenstein*. Mary had read three of his four best novels before writing her own: *Edgar Huntley* (1799) in 1814, and in 1815 both *Ormond* (1799) and *Wieland* (1798).[43] Like *Frankenstein*, Brown's work belongs to the tradition of explained or naturalistic gothic, a second generation characteristic of the genre. Typically, Brown reveals unsuspected psychic or physical abilities to be the source of apparently supernatural phenomena.

Wieland in particular seems to have been a source of inspiration for Mary. Aside from the concern with incest which Brown's novel shares with *Frankenstein* and the gothic novel generally, there is also the presence of a physically unappealing figure named Carwin who has a talent for ventriloquism.[44] The exercising of this talent has frightening consequences leading Carwin to the reflection which, as F. C. Prescott first suggested, may have provided the germinal idea for *Frankenstein*: "had I not rashly set in motion a machine, over whose progress I had no controul, and which experience has shown me was infinite in power? Every day might add to the catalogue of horrors of which this was the source . . . "[45] However this may be, another of Brown's novels did contribute to one of Mary's: the epidemic in *Arthur Mervyn* (1799-1800) was an influence on *The Last Man* (1826).[46]

29

Without doubt *Frankenstein* would not exist at all but for the background of the gothic novel with its emphasis on generally horrific but always vivid sensations, suppressed sexuality and Faustian villains. Brown was but one of the more famous practitioners of the genre with whose works Mary was familiar. She read Anne Radcliffe's *The Italian* (1797) in 1814, her *Mysteries of Udolpho* (1794) in 1815 and William Beckford's *Vathek* (1786) in 1815.[47] Shelley's two early efforts in this direction—*Zastrozzi* (1809)[48] and *St. Irvine, or The Rosicrucian* (1810)—might also be counted as likely influences. In hot pursuit of the mysteries of life and death, the protagonist of *St. Irvine* is, like Godwin's St. Leon, cursed with eternal life. The gothic novel is often related to the dark and depraved side of Romanticism as exemplified in the writings of de Sade. There is no evidence that Mary read his *Justine* (1791), but Mario Praz draws attention to the coincidental presence of someone called Justine in the role of an innocent victim in *Frankestein*.[49] What is clear, however, is that before beginning *Frankenstein* and radically modifying the conventions of the gothic genre (for example, substituting for a distant vaguely medieval locale something more contemporary[50]), Mary had a thorough knowledge of those conventions.

Interestingly enough, during that summer of 1816 the famous gothic novelist, "Monk" Lewis visited Diodati and told a number of horror stories. But that was after *Frankenstein* was well under way. However, Mary had read his famous novel, *The Monk* (1796), on the evening of September 22, 1814.[51] Furthermore, it is possible, as Walter Peck suggests, that the names "Frankheim" and "Falkenstein" which appear in Lewis's *Romantic Tales* (1808) may have combined in Mary's mind to form the name Frankenstein.[52]

Frankenstein is remarkable for the way in which it transcends the limitations of the conventional gothic novel and encompasses the concerns of Romanticism at large. It is not surprising, therefore, that some of the major Romantic poems are either directly quoted in the pages of *Frankenstein* or present as possible sources of inspiration. Some lines from Wordsworth's "Tintern Abbey" are appropriated by Frankenstein to describe Clerval's passionate response to the natural environment but, of the Romantic poems relevant to Mary's novel, the most important is Coleridge's *The Ancient Mariner*. It provides an analogue at least for Mary's use of the polar setting. Walton attributes his interest in "the dangerous mysteries of ocean" to his reading of that poem. As he tells his sister, "I am going to unexplored regions, to 'the land of mist and snow,' but I shall kill no albatross; therefore do not be alarmed for my safety or if I should come back to you as worn and woeful as the 'Ancient Mariner'" (p. 21). Actually, Walton's role more closely approximates Coleridge's Wedding Guest as he listens to Frankenstein's extraordinary tale. It is Frankenstein who finds himself akin to the Ancient Mariner with a "deadly weight yet hanging around my neck, and bowing me to the ground" (pp. 151-52) and "haunted by a curse that shut up every avenue to enjoyment" (p. 154).

Frankenstein's nightmare, in which he embraces his mother's corpse, may owe something to Byron's reading a manuscript copy of Coleridge's *Christabel*, an event that preceded his proposing the ghost-story competitions.[53] The witch Geraldine, the description of whose deformed breasts inspired Shelley's horrifying vision of a woman with eyes for nipples, seems to be related to Christabel's dead mother who made a death-bed promise to return. Marc A. Rubenstein wonders if the unacknowledged indebtedness to Coleridge here caused Mary to compensate with the footnoted quotation from *The Ancient Mariner* in the episode immediately following.[54] In flight from the monster who appeared by his bedside displacing the dream of his dead mother, Frankenstein is reminded, like the Mariner, of one who walks in "fear and dread," "Because he knows a frightful fiend/Doth close behind him tread" (p. 59).

Between May and July 4, 1816, while at Villa Diodati, Byron began and completed the Third Canto of *Childe Harold* and gave it to Mary to read.[55] The scenic backdrop is as important to his Canto as it is to Mary's novel and the spirit of Childe Harold's reaction to the Alps is identical to Frankenstein's

> Above me are the Alps,
> The palace of Nature, whose vast walls
> Have pinnacled in clouds their snowy scalps,
> And throned Eternity in icy halls
> Of cold sublimity, where forms and falls
> The avalanche—the thunderbolt of snow!
> All that expands the spirit, yet appals
> Gather around these summits, as to show
> How Earth may pierce to Heaven, yet leave vain man below.[56]

The storm which Frankenstein witnesses on returning to Geneva from Ingolstadt appears to owe something to the storm which Byron witnessed on June 13, 1816, and which became part of Childe Harold's experience. After leaving Lausanne where the snowy mountains are described with a phrase from *Childe Harold* as "the palaces of nature" (p. 74),[57] Mary has Frankenstein come across the monster momentarily illuminated by shafts of lightning so that he appears suddenly in different locations; one flash "discovered him to be hanging among the rocks of the nearly perpendicular ascent of Mont Salêve" (p. 76). In Byron's poem,

Far along,
From peak to peak, the rattling crags among
Leaps the live thunder![58]

Seemingly, the monster bounds about like Byron's thunder. It also appears likely that the character of Frankenstein is loosely related to the Byronic hero as exemplified by Childe Harold himself and more particularly by the eponymous Promethean hero of *Manfred*, the drama that Byron began in the summer of 1816.

As a final literary source, it is reasonable to assume that Mary derived much from the work of her lover and husband, Percy Bysshe Shelley. In calling the monster "daemon" and in suggesting that he is one aspect of a doppelgänger pair involved in an ambiguous mutual pursuit, Mary is paralleling prominent obsessions in Shelley's poetry. Some of the more problematic elements in this literary relationship—the similarities between Shelley's "Mont Blanc" and Mary's metaphoric use of the Alps, and Mary's attitude towards Shelley's philosophical position—will be discussed in detail in Chapters 4 and 5. For the moment I wish only to indicate that, of the poems of Shelley which were available to Mary in the summer of 1816, "Alastor, or the Spirit of Solitude" is clearly of most relevance to the concerns of *Frankenstein*. In the words of Shelley's Preface to the poem, it is about a youthful Poet who "drinks deep of the fountains of knowledge, and is still insatiate." But intellectual obsession has its limitations and eventually the Poet "thirsts for intercourse with an intelligence similar to itself."[59] He imagines an ideal woman who is somehow commensurate with everything that he finds beautiful and mysterious in the external universe. Unable and basically unwilling to find a corresponding reality for this image, the Poet wastes away. Since the Poet is unable to appreciate a reality beyond himself, the landscape throughout is that created by the condition of his own mind. The general affinity between the Poet and Frankenstein is obvious enough but it is in the details of Shelley's poetic embodiment that the most striking similarities occur.

In pursuit of knowledge, the Poet has slept "In charnels and on coffins."[60] On one occasion while he sleeps, he dreams of his ideal, the embrace of "a veilèd maid" singing of "Knowledge and truth and virtue."[61] At this point he awakes. This dream may be one of several sources for the dream in which Frankenstein believes himself to be embracing Elizabeth only to awake in horror when the image of Elizabeth metamorphoses into that of his dead mother, her lips "livid with the hue of death" (p. 58). The nightmarish conclusion of the Poet's dream is withheld until the end of the poem where the reader is invited to regard the corpse of the Poet with its "pallid lips." But

32

although Frankenstein sees "the grave worms crawling in the folds" (p. 58) of his mother's death shroud, the Poet is "Yet safe from the worm's outrage."[62]

This image of metamorphosis brings my survey of literary sources and analogues full circle to join with Ovid's *Metamorphoses* where I began. It hardly seems accidental that the only lines of Shelley's which are actually quoted in *Frankenstein* (p. 98) derive from his poem "Mutability." And, of course, what is significant about the material Mary has appropriated for *Frankenstein* is the way it is transformed, metamorphosed in that context.

(ii) *Aspects of Actuality*

A concentric arrangement, similar to that employed in *Frankenstein*, suggests itself as the most logical way to organize visually those elements from the "real world" which seem to have contributed to Mary's masterpiece. The outer ring consists of various relevant aspects of the world at large with which Mary either came in contact or about which she may have had some knowledge. As one would expect, however, this material is of essentially peripheral interest. More pertinent is the use Mary made of her biographical circumstances. A consideration of the extent to which *Frankenstein* can be understood in terms of Shelley and the other famous figures with whom Mary was related or associated is offered in my inner ring of factual influences. But of greatest value in elucidating some of *Frankenstein*'s darker corners, and at the core of this concentric system, are whatever "facts" can be intuited about Mary's psychological drives.

As we have seen, Mary might have had some knowledge of the mythical history of the mechanical man, but something approaching the actuality—the automaton—did exist in Mary's time and must be counted amongst her "real world" influences. In 1814, when Mary and Shelley eloped to the Continent they stopped (from August 19 to August 21) in Neuchâtel where, between 1710 and 1773, the kind of intricate ingenuity the Swiss put into the manufacture of watches had been directed into the creation of mechanisms resembling the shape and mimicking the movement of the human figure. Automata were created that exhibited all kinds of accomplishments including dancing, drawing and playing chess. But it was a Frenchman, Jacques de Vaucanson, who came closest to being la Mettrie's "nouveau Prométhée." His creations are miracles of fidelity.[63]

If Mary was influenced by these automata, it is only appropriate that many commentators have distortedly viewed Frankenstein's organic monster as the major precursor of science fiction's robots, androids and other intelligent machines. Herman Melville seems to have been the first to connect Mary's conception with the construction of a mechanical man. He has Ahab in *Moby-Dick* interrupt the *Pequod*'s carpenter with the line, "Hold; while Prometheus is about it, I'll order a complete man after a desirable pattern,"[64] whereupon he provides a detailed blue-print for an iron man. It is unlikely that Melville would have had Ahab call the carpenter "Prometheus" without the example of Mary's *Modern Prometheus*. And he had, in fact, acquired a copy of *Frankenstein* in December, 1849. Some years later, he published a tale entitled "The Bell Tower" (1855) which is clearly indebted to *Frankenstein*.[65] The protagonist, Bannadonna, a Promethean over-reacher, who has manufactured a wonderful automaton which he names Talus, is killed by his own creation.

Whether or not Mary came across automatons while eloping in 1814, Radu Florescu does believe that during that period abroad Mary visited or at least heard about Castle Frankenstein near Darmstadt, Germany.[66] Whatever reasons might be adduced for the appropriateness of Mary's choosing the name Frankenstein, Florescu argues that she would not have originally chosen it but for knowledge of the place itself. After all, Frankenstein never was a particularly common German name and now, like the name Hitler, it must be virtually extinct. It is part of Florescu's argument to demonstrate that Castle Frankenstein's legendary associations concerning an alchemist and a dragon-slaying knight might well be aligned with Mary's tale. An alchemist named Johann Konrad Dippel registered himself as a "Frankensteiner" at the University of Giessen because he was born at Castle Frankenstein in 1673. Although the case for Dippel as a model for Frankenstein seems tenuous, it is possible that, when Mary thought of her story of a man with alchemical interests, the name of Frankenstein came to mind because of the Dippel connection. As for the dragon-slaying legend, first recorded in the *Deutsche Sagen* (1816-18) of the brothers Grimm, it is clearly a variant of the St. George and the dragon story with a resident of Castle Frankenstein in the St. George role. But equally clearly, it cannot be paralleled with Mary's narrative in any significant sense. However, in the 1818 edition of *Frankenstein*, St. George himself does figure amongst a series of figures around whom the child Clerval was wont to compose plays.[67] Nevertheless, although different sources of inspiration are offered in the 1831 text, it would be absurd to argue that Mary was covering up one of her own sources of inspiration.

Florescu does resort to a cover-up argument to explain why Mary, having visited Castle Frankenstein, expunged the event from both the *Journal* and her *History of a Six Week's Tour* (1817), and failed to mention it in the Introduction describing the genesis of *Frankenstein*.[68] But did Mary ever visit the place? The only piece of circumstantial evidence is the entry in

Mary's *Journal* for September 2, 1814. On their way back to England, she and Shelley are sailing down the Rhine:

> We arrive at Manheim early in the morning; breakfast there; the town is clean and good. We proceeded towards Mayence [Mainz] with an unfavourable wind; towards evening the batelier rests just as the wind changes in our favour. Mary and Shelley walk for three hours; they are alone. At 11 we depart. We sleep in the boat.[69]

Castle Frankenstein is situated 8 or 9 miles east of the Rhine between Mannheim and Mainz. It is possible but unlikely that the three hour walk from an unspecified anchorage (maybe an island near Gernsheim which is mentioned in the corresponding portion of Clair's *Journal*[70]) was to Castle Frankenstein and back.

My own view—and it rests upon evidence (that Florescu does not take note of) within the text of *Frankenstein* rather than any external documentation—is that Mary probably did somehow get to know of Castle Frankenstein but did not physically go there. On the way to England, Frankenstein and Clerval retrace the trip which Mary and Shelley made down the Rhine. They stay at Mannheim and after passing Mainz (rather than before, where Castle Frankenstein is actually situated),

> We saw many ruined castles standing on the edges of precipices, surrounded by black woods, high and inaccessible. This part of the Rhine, indeed, presents a singularly varigated landscape. In one spot you view rugged hills, ruined castles overlooking tremendous precipices, with the dark Rhine rushing beneath; and, on the sudden turn of a promontary, flourishing vineyards with green sloping banks, and a meandering river, and populous towns occupy the scene. (p. 155)

Clerval then relates and distinguishes this scene from those he is familiar with in Switzerland: "The mountains of Switzerland are more majestic and strange; but there is a charm in the banks of this divine river, that I never before saw equalled. Look at that castle which overhangs yon precipice; and that also on the island ... and now that group of labourers coming from among their vines; and that village half hid in the recess of the mountain" (p. 156).[71]

Clerval apparently thinks that the majestic scenery of Switzerland is not set off by the homely as is the scenery viewed from the Rhine. But, in fact, on an earlier occasion when Frankenstein, in the company of Clerval in the 1818 text, alone in that of 1831, is travelling in Switzerland towards his *Mer de Glace* confrontation with the monster, the scene more or less parallels the majestic homely mix of the Rhinelands—and there are castles. In the words of the 1818 text, identical to those published in 1831 except for the pronouns,

35

"as we ascended still higher, the valley assumed a more magnificent and astonishing character. Ruined castles hanging on the precipices of piny mountains; the impetuous Arve, and cottages every here and there peeping forth from among the trees, formed a scene of singular beauty."[72] This "picturesque" valley of Servox gives way to the "sublime" valley of Chamonix where there are "no more ruined castles and fertile fields" (p. 95).[73]

This is one of three striking occasions in *Frankenstein* where the elements of one scene reappear slightly transmogrified in another. In this case, it is as if the scenery of the Rhine is superimposed on the scenery of the Arve, or vice versa. Is this Mary's way of indicating the relevance of her experiences while journeying down the Rhine in 1814 to what occurs in the Alpine setting of *Frankenstein*? Is this a way of transposing Castle Frankenstein to the Alps? What matter if the location of the castles which Frankenstein and Clerval observe while sailing down the Rhine does not quite coincide with that of the actual Castle Frankenstein? Mary's art, as I have indicated, is a matter of metamorphosis. Not only do the books and experiences which Mary drew on become plastic and undergo a process of metamorphosis in becoming part of *Frankenstein* but, within the context of the book itself, one episode or one element seems to be assimilated metamorphically into another.

Also while eloping in 1814, Mary came across some information which, almost certainly, explains why the university that Frankenstein attends is situated in Ingolstadt. Shelley had bought a copy of Barruel's four-volume *Memoirs Illustrating the History of Jacobinism* (1797-98), translated by R. Clifford. Two of the volumes give an account of the Illuminists, a secret international society seeking the creation of a secular, egalitarian society through world revolution, which was founded by Dr. Adam Weishaupt in May, 1776, in Ingolstadt. While crossing Lake Lucerne in Switzerland, Shelley, Mary and her step-sister, Jane (subsequently known as Claire), read about the Illuminists. Both Mary and Jane record that they studied Barruel's *History* over the three days following.[74]

Since the monster comes into being in a city associated with a revolutionary conspiracy, perhaps Freudian interpretations of *Frankenstein* should be made over into, or combined with, Marxist ones. After all, if the monster can be associated with unconscious ideas, it is but a small step to equate repressed levels of mind with the lower classes, the revolutionary masses. This Darko Suvin does, suggesting that the botched monster is analogous to the botched French Revolution.[75] Certainly, if Mary is commenting on the French Revolution, she is displaying yet another general symptom of Romanticism. I believe that the ideas with which Mary is dealing in *Frankenstein* are at a level of generality which makes them applicable to all aspects of life. *Franken-*

stein is not primarily about political revolution but it does occasionally appear that such a dimension is annexed to ideas and ambitions which are overall more philosophical and abstract.

First of all, it should be observed that the events of *Frankenstein* may be occurring in the 1790's, the decade of the French Revolution. Walton's letters are dated ambiguously in the year 17—. It should also be observed that while in Oxford, Frankenstein and Clerval visit the tomb of John Hampden, Cromwell's cousin and a Parliamentary hero killed during the Civil War: "For a moment my soul was elevated from its debasing and miserable fears, to contemplate the divine ideas of liberty and self-sacrifice, of which these sights were the monuments and the remembrancers. For an instant I dared to shake off my chains, and look around me with a free and lofty spirit; but the iron had eaten into my flesh, and I sank again, trembling and hopeless, into my miserable self" (p. 160). Perhaps Mary is here insinuating a disenchantment with the idea of revolution itself. She was, in fact, politically conservative and William A. Walling has gone so far as to suggest that the plague in *The Last Man* represents the nature and consequences of egalitarian ideas.[76] Frankenstein's desire for "some mighty revolution that might bury me and my betrayer in its ruins" (p. 182) can be read as implying that in a revolution both sides lose. It might be noted, in addition, that the book by Volney which Felix used to teach Safie English is a translation from a French original, the full title of which is *Les Ruines, ou méditations sur les révolutions des empires* (1791).

Mary seems to have had little sympathy with the visions of a grand new world which characteristically inspire revolutions. There is a vision of a spiritual new world in *Frankenstein* but that, it is recognized, may be an illusion, and the only reality, the New World of North America, is a bleak alternative. It is never alluded to in any positive fashion. Frankenstein envisages his monster supplied with a mate leaving Europe to "inhabit the deserts of the new world" and procreate "a race of devils" (p. 165). Within the North American context, the monster's role, like Caliban's in *The Tempest*, corresponds with that of the Indian. Thus, overhearing Felix read from Volney's *Ruins of Empire*, the monster learnt "of the discovery of the American hemisphere, and wept with Safie over the hapless fate of its original inhabitants" (p. 119).

A consideration of the relevance of Illuminism, the French Revolution and revolution generally in *Frankenstein* provides a natural point of transfer from my outer ring of "real world" influences to the inner ring, the influence of the people with whom Mary was intimately associated, particularly Shelley. Unlike Mary, Shelley enthusiastically favoured political revolution through-

37

out his life. The argument that Frankenstein is based on Shelley can only be bolstered by associating Frankenstein's creation with political ambitions of a revolutionary kind. P. D. Fleck provides the first extended demonstration that Frankenstein is a portrait of Shelley.[77] He argues that the negative valuation of Frankenstein is consistent with the disapproval of Shelley's abstract idealism which Mary reveals in her notes to his poems. Recently, Christopher Small has taken the space of a book—*Ariel Like a Harpy*—to present a similar case without, however, any reference to Fleck's article. In this context the case can be presented rather more briefly.

To some degree, the development of Frankenstein's alchemical and scientific interests parallel Shelley's. It is perhaps worth mentioning that, describing a visit to Oxford in 1815 with Shelley and Mary, Charles Clairmont wrote to his sister Claire that "We visited the very rooms where the two noted infidels, Shelley and Hogg (now, happily, excluded from the society of the present residents), pored, with the incessant and unwearied application of the alchemist, over the certified and natural boundaries of human knowledge."[78] It is at this point that Shelley's history coincides with Friar Bacon's and the association may well have been in Mary's mind when, as we have seen, in one of the manuscript fragments, she introduces a visit to rooms once occupied by someone she mistakenly calls "Chancellor" Bacon. Small suggests that Frankenstein derived his Christian name from the fact that the volume of poems published by Shelley and his sister Elizabeth in 1810, Shelley's first publication, are offered pseudonymously as "by Victor and Cazire." Small also points out that the hero of an early poem, "The Wandering Jew" (1810), is called Victoria, that a burlesque of Shelley's, also published in 1810 while he was at Oxford, is purportedly by "John Fitzvictor," that a victim in *St. Irvine* is called Victoria, and that the words "victory," "victor" and "victorious" recur in his poetry.[79] Furthermore, the fact that Shelley's early co-author, Elizabeth, was his favourite sister and the closest of his childhood friends seems pertinent to the relationship between Frankenstein and his "cousin" Elizabeth.

The narrative pattern of flight and pursuit in *Frankenstein* might also be related to Shelley's career. In both cases, flight is often indistinguishable from pursuit suggesting that both Shelley and Frankenstein are attempting to dodge a demon within. Small seizes on an appropriate metaphor when he equates the fleeing Shelley with Shakespeare's Ariel (the preferred name, not incidentally, of the boat in which Shelley died) and the inner demon, Frankenstein's monster, with the corresponding figure of Caliban, or, in the words of a stage direction in *The Tempest*, "Ariel, like a Harpy."[80] Unlike Mary, Shelley favoured the contemplation of his visions of a transcendent utopia rather than confrontation with the nastier aspects of his own mind and the world around him. For Small, this contrast is epitomized by relating *Frankenstein* to *Prometheus Unbound* as alternate elaborations of the same metaphor, the one negative, the other positive. My own reading of *Frankenstein* does not disallow its being read as an attack on Shelley's Romantic idealism but such an interpretation is, I believe, radically incomplete.

There is one event in Shelley's biography which is of particular relevance to *Frankenstein*. While staying with his first wife Harriet and her sister Eliza Westbrook at a cottage name Tan-yr-alt (Under-the-Hill) near the Welsh village of Tremadoc, Shelley believed that he was shot at by an unknown assailant on the night of February 26, 1813. Several of Shelley's biographers have dismissed the incident as one of his hallucinations, although Richard Holmes, the most recent biographer, argues rather convincingly on the basis of the feelings of hostility aroused in the community by Shelley's radical views that the attack was real.[81] According to Harriet's account of the incident in a letter, dated March 12, to the bookseller, Thomas Hookham, after Shelley had returned his attacker's fire, the man "said these words: By God, I will be revenged! I will murder your wife. I will ravish your sister. By God, I will be revenged!"[82] This threat strikingly anticipates that of Frankenstein's monster: "I shall be with you on your wedding-night" (p. 168). Subsequently, Shelley supposedly drew a picture of his attacker on a wooden fire screen. The screen has been destroyed or lost but a copy made by Miss Fanny Holland (reproduced following this page) shows one of Shelley's demonic figures grinning at a window. It seems more than coincidental that when Frankenstein first sees the monster at his Orkneys laboratory it is as "the daemon at the casement" (p. 166)—"casement" being Shelley's substitution for Mary's "window"—and, after Elizabeth's strangulation,[83] Frankenstein "saw at the open window a figure the most hideous and abhorred. A grin was on the face of the monster; he seemed to jeer, as with his fiendish finger he pointed towards the corpse. . . . " Frankenstein "rushed towards the window, and drawing a pistol" (p. 196) fired, but without effect. Shelley had also fired through a window at what he saw as a retreating figure.

Small does make most of the connections here[84] but he fails to mention a further detail which appears to be related. When the Shelleys first arrived in Wales, characteristically in flight from difficulties in England, wild rumours were flying around concerning the murderer of a farm-house maid who had been hacked to death. A giant of a man, over six feet tall, he was known as "the King of the Mountains."[85] It seems likely that this "giant" became assimilated in Shelley's mind with his assailant and that, in turn, this compilation attached itself to Mary's conception of Frankenstein's monster.

39

SHELLEY'S TAN-YR-ALT ASSAILANT

From Shelley's sketch as copied by Miss Fanny Holland, and published in the Century Magazine, *October 1905*

40

Of course this kind of biographical explanation of a literary text is highly conjectural at best. Thus, on the one hand, it might be argued that the persona of Shelley is divided between Frankenstein and the more poetic Clerval. On the other hand, the name Clerval suggests Claire Clairmont with the substitution of a valley for a mountain. The equation with Claire is further supported by the fact that in a letter to Byron (she was his insecure mistress), letting him know she was on the way to Geneva, Claire told him to address letters to her as "Clairville" so as not to invoke ugly memories of her mother, Mary Jane Clairmont.[86] Are we to infer that the relationship between Elizabeth, Frankenstein and Clerval is triangular like that between Mary, Shelley and Claire? And what about Byron? To what extent is Frankenstein a Byronic hero based on the man himself? Alternatively, the fact that Mary admired Byron's realism[87] may have something to do with the apparently negative appraisal of Frankenstein's idealism. At the same time, it should be observed that Frankenstein's younger brother, William, who is "very tall of his age, with sweet laughing blue eyes, dark eyelashes, and curling hair," might almost be a portrait of Byron as a child. He already has "one or two little *wives*, but Louisa Biron is his favourite ... " (p. 66). Like the other sources of *Frankenstein*, those of a biographical nature undergo a startling process of shift and metamorphosis.

Of the various human portraits that may be glimpsed in *Frankenstein*, none is more interesting than the portrait that Mary presents of herself. We now, it would appear, cross the divide between external and internal influences and enter that central core circumscribed by Mary Shelley's own skull. But here, as so frequently in *Frankenstein* itself, the distinction between inner and outer is chimerical. After all, whether Mary is drawing on her sense of the French Revolution or her sense of her own husband, she is, in fact, limning the contours of her own mind. Surprisingly enough, given the unique nature of Mary's creation, it is only very recently that critics have looked at *Frankenstein* for signs of its author's psychological profile. Needless to say, this is an area where the mere critic, whether he be psychoanalytically informed or not, must tread with extreme caution.

What, for example, are we to make of the emphasis on incestuous relationships in *Frankenstein*.[88] To be sure, the flavour of incest is a generic characteristic of the gothic novel but that does not preclude a personal interest on Mary's part. Perhaps she was aware of an incestuous element in her feelings for her father? In her autobiographical novella, *Mathilda*, written in 1819 but not published in her lifetime because of her father's disapproval, the love of Mathilda and her father is imaged as "this monster with whom none might mingle in converse."[89] Not only did Mary dedicate *Frankenstein* to her father but she named her first son William after him. It seems all the more extraordinary, an act of prescient masochism, that she gave the same name to the boy who is the monster's first victim. Perhaps something of Mary's conflicting feelings here may be gauged if it is recalled that Mary had a younger half-brother, also named William, of whom she may well have been jealous.

It has recently been proposed by Ellen Moers that much in *Frankenstein* is to be explained in terms of Mary's horror of childbirth.[90] Her own mother died when she was born, and her own baby girl, born two months prematurely on February 22nd, 1815, died within two weeks on March 6th.[91] Perhaps the idea of an artificially created human being appealed to Mary as a way of avoiding the normal biological process. Her pathetic *Journal* entry for March 19, 1815, is surely relevant: "Dream that my little baby came to life again; that it had only been cold, and that we rubbed it before the fire, and it lived. Awake and find no baby."[92] It will be recalled that a subsequent "dream" of animation, that recorded in the 1831 Introduction, provided Mary with the subject matter of *Frankenstein*. In that same introduction, Mary refers to her novel as "my hideous progeny" (p. 10), sufficient indication it might seem, of the way in which literary production and biological reproduction were entwined in her mind. For Moers the hideous nature of Frankenstein's creation and his destructive career reflect the grotesque juxtaposition of birth and death in Mary's own experience. But the monster is also presented in a contrary role as a "piteous victim of parental abandonment"[93] and that too might be related to Mary's own experience, her sense of being deserted by her mother.

This last aspect is brilliantly explored by Marc A. Rubenstein whose speculative article caps if it does not eclipse Moers' account. At the heart of an ingenious argument, the details of which I shall not attempt to reproduce, is the notion that *Frankenstein*'s concentric narrative arrangement implies a structural pole that is symbolically equivalent to the polar conclusion. At the centre of a series of receding narrative frames (the outermost of which is conceived as the account of the novel's genesis offered in the Introduction) is the story of Safie's mother who, like all the other mothers in the book, is dead:

> Safie related that her mother was a Christian Arab, seized and made a slave by the Turks; recommended by her beauty, she had won the heart of the father of Safie, who married her. The young girl spoke in high and enthusiastic terms of her mother, who, born in freedom, spurned the bondage to which she was now reduced. She instructed her daughter in the tenets of her religion, and taught her to aspire to higher powers of intellect,

and an independence of spirit, forbidden to the female followers of Muhammad. This lady died; but her lessons were indelibly impressed on the mind of Safie ... (pp. 123-24).

"This," opines Rubenstein (and the point, once stated, seems so plausible it is extraordinary that 158 years had to go by before it was made), "is surely a cartoon, distorted but recognizable, of the author's mother, Mary Wollstonecraft."[94] This area of warmth, Safie's mother in a harem, at the novel's structural pole corresponds to the area of warmth and light which Walton fantasizes as existing at the earth's geographical north pole. There is both an outward physical momentum in *Frankenstein* and an inner psychological one but ultimately, like the exterior pole and the interior pole, the one demands to be understood in terms of the other. Rubenstein explains hints in the book at the Hyperborean myth of a warm polar womb (suggested by the promised conjunction of fire and ice and by the aural pun on mother and sea in the *Mer de Glace*) in terms of Mary's guilty interest in her own conception and her search for her own mother in the sea of ice.

Some of the more startling details of Rubenstein's case gain in credibility from the persuasiveness of his general drift. For example, it does seem at least possible that the monster's awareness of the "disgusting circumstances" of his "accursed origin" (p. 130), gained from the papers he had taken from Frankenstein's laboratory (a revelation heralded by what Rubenstein calls a narrative "perturbation" when, a few pages earlier, the monster refers to copies he has made of Safie's letters to Felix), corresponds to Mary's knowledge of the love letters that her mother-to-be wrote to Godwin. And it does seem weirdly coincidental that what Rubenstein sees as an observed primal scene, when the monster is imbued with life, should occur in November—the month in which Mary was conceived. Another narrative "perturbation" is also revealing. In searching for the secret of life, Frankenstein likens himself to "the Arabian who had been buried with the dead, and found a passage to life, aided only by one glimmering, and seemingly ineffectual, light" (p. 53). The allusion is to the *Arabian Nights* and the fifth voyage of Sinbad where he finds himself buried, according to local custom, with his dead wife, but there is also an important connection to be made here with another "Arabian," Safie, "who seems to point to the 'mother' at the structural center of the novel."[95] It is also, of course, significant that *Christabel*, the poem which Mary heard Lord Byron read,[96] seems to be about the return of a mother who died while giving birth.

Rubenstein provides one further series of associations which is of particular interest. The fact, he speculates, that Jane was pregnant at the time of *Frankenstein*'s initial stages of composition may have reminded Mary of her own pregnancy and of the horrific context, recorded by Shelley in the *Journal*, in which he announced that pregnancy to Jane. (Here, it should be observed, is one of those occasions where it is inappropriate to distinguish between textual and actual influences.) On the evening of October 7, 1814, Shelley had succeeded in terrifying Jane with one of his ghost stories: "her countenance ... beamed with a deadly whiteness ... her hair became prominent and erect; her eyes were wide and staring, drawn almost from the sockets by the convulsions of the muscles; the eyelids were forced in, and the eyeballs, without any relief, seemed as if they had been newly inserted, in ghastly sport, in the sockets of a lifeless head ... I informed her of Mary's pregnancy." As one might expect, this information did not bring Jane out of her horrified state; rather it intensified it, causing her to react with "the most dreadful convulsions."[97] Possibly, Mary had this *Journal* entry at least subliminally in mind while describing the "convulsive motion" (p. 57) with which the monster came to life (in a scene simulating intercourse and orgasm) and his horrifying face. As Rubenstein notes, "Shelley made of Jane's face a kind of composite corpse"[98] and the detail of the "newly inserted" eyeball finds its echo in that of the monster's "watery eyes ... the same colour as the dun-white sockets in which they were set" (p. 57).

However, in the context of Rubenstein's reading that monster is to be identified not so much with Jane Clairmont as with Mary Shelley. Consequently, Frankenstein is to be identified (again at least subliminally) with Mary Wollstonecraft. As I have indicated, Mary's choice of the name Frankenstein has been the subject of some controversy, a controversy to which may be added a further hypothesis. I suspect that Mary Shelley was, at times, equally preoccupied with the unusual name Wollstonecraft and believe it likely that she was drawn to the name Frankenstein because it reproduces some of the features of her mother's surname. The "stone" in Wollstonecraft translated into German becomes the "stein" in Frankenstein. Etymologically, the forms of the two names are similar. Wollstonecraft derives from Wulfstan's croft or dwelling, Frankenstein from the castle—admittedly a less modest dwelling—of the Franks or French. But "Frank" in German also means free, an idea which is also present in the English word "frank." Thus it would appear that Mary Wollstonecraft could appropriately be regarded as "frank" in both German and English.

CHAPTER THREE

Thematic Anatomy:
Intrinsic Structures

The materials examined in the previous chapter might be described as centrifugal in orientation. An understanding of their significance involves a flight into areas outside the text of *Frankenstein*. Of course, within the text, not all that may be known about these materials is operational or of equal weight. There are centripetal or gravitational forces holding the text together which cause its component parts to assume certain lines of coherence. An identification of these lines of coherence will reveal the book's thematic anatomy. My terminology here makes the parallel with Frankenstein's construct self-evident. Once having decided on the creation of a human being, Frankenstein worked within a particular system of organization.

A distinction should be made between the idea content and the thematic content of a work. While an idea is essentially something static, a theme must involve process and development. Obviously enough, in the case of *Franken-stein*, the central idea presented itself in Mary's vision—the Lazarus-like raising to life of an artificially created man. The transition from idea to extended and successful narrative requires a "vertical" testing of exactly what the idea means in a number of different contexts and a "horizontal" exploration of its possible consequences in human action and response. What is of thematic interest will derive largely but not exclusively from the horizontal axis. The vertical potential should be considered as part of the idea context and will receive more emphasis in the next two chapters.

In considering the basic idea of *Frankenstein*, Mary Shelley saw two implications that allowed for thematic development. First of all, the subject raised the question of the "I" and the "not-I," the alien, the Other. From this point of view, Frankenstein's relationship with the monster becomes analogous with the other relationships in the book. The monster becomes an extreme instance of the Other. After all, the monster concept is a relative one and, since it is only meaningful from a human perspective, the human and the monstrous might be understood as enjoying a symbiotic existence. Perhaps some such reflection prompted the second implication, the logical step of treating the monster as Frankenstein's doppelgänger. These two secondary ideas, vertical elaborations, presented the major possibilities for the thematic lines of development traced in detail below. It will be immediately apparent that these lines of development combine either antagonistically or paradoxically. While the first emphasizes the reality of the Other, the second tends to validate nothing beyond the I.

(i) *Egotistic Perversion and Domestic Affection*

Frankenstein, like many artists and scientists, becomes involved in his work to the extent that the external world of nature and human relationships loses its influence. In his solitary cell "at the top of the house, and separated from all other apartments by a gallery and staircase"—an architectural analogue for the divorce of mind and body—he is oblivious to the processes of nature evident outside during an unusually prolific summer: "never did the fields bestow a more plentiful harvest or the vines yield a more luxuriant vintage" (p. 55). He ceases communication with his friends and family. At the same time, Frankenstein does appear to accept the reproach he attributes in imagination to his father: "If the study to which you apply yourself has a tendency to weaken your affections, and to destroy your taste for those simple pleasures in which no alloy can mix, then that study is certainly unlawful, that is to say, not befitting the human mind" (p. 56).

This moment of awareness and self-condemnation on Frankenstein's part is not without equivocation. He continues: "if no man allowed any pursuit whatsoever to interfere with the tranquility of his domestic affections, Greece had not been enslaved; Caesar would have spared his country; America would would have been discovered more gradually; and the empires of Mexico and Peru had not been destroyed" (p. 56). The reader will observe that these instances include an odd-man-out. We have observed Mary's negative appraisal of the New World but the perhaps too rapid discovery of America is not an evil equal in magnitude to the other three examples, if it was indeed an evil at all (whether the discovery had been fast or slow it may be assumed that the Indian would have suffered). Here as elsewhere Mary is posing a question, not forcing a clear-cut conclusion.

At the tale's conclusion, after all the deaths and misery arising out of Frankenstein's creation, the same mixed judgement is upheld. When some of the sailors aboard the ice-locked ship seek to persuade Robert Walton, their captain and Frankenstein's rescuer, to return home, Frankenstein arouses in them a sense of the glory of their mission. In words that express his own ambitions, he reminds the sailors of their expectation "to be hailed as the benefactors of your species" (p. 214). And as part of a speech that echoes that of Dante's Ulysses, Frankenstein exhorts: "Do not return to your families with the stigma of disgrace marked on your brows. Return, as heroes who have fought and conquered and who know not what it is to turn their backs on the foe" (p. 215). But, as we have seen, the allusion is ironically employed; the voyage that Ulysses persuades his sailors to undertake is fatal. Hence his place amongst the flame-enveloped evil counsellors. Is Frankenstein condemning himself once again? His death-bed advice to Walton shortly afterwards would appear to indicate that this is so: "Seek happiness in tranquility and avoid ambition, even if it be only the innocent one of distinguishing yourself in science and discoveries." But immediately he reverses his position: "Yet why do I say this! I have myself been blasted in these hopes, yet another may succeed" (pp. 217-218).

One is left with a divided impression of Frankenstein exactly parallel to that provided by the conclusion of Marlowe's *Doctor Faustus*. The presentation of the final moments before Faustus's damnation has left commentators confused as to where Marlowe, the atheist, stands. The evidence for ambivalence and ironic undercutting here is a good deal more subtle than it is in *Frankenstein*'s case and, indeed, some critics have denied its existence. But to my mind a convincing argument can be made that Marlowe is manipulating the traditional story in order to point up his admiration for Faustus and question the justice of his damnation. In the case of Mary's comparable sympathy for Frankenstein, it is likely, given the analogy between the book and the monster, that it has much to do with the fact that writing involves the same isolation and perhaps a similar twisting of the sexual impulse as Frankenstein's occupation. And like the writer, Frankenstein sees in his work the promise of immortality.

The relationship between creativity and sexual energy is something of a metaphoric if not a scientific cliché. Regarding the success of his initial experiments at animating dead matter, Frankenstein notes, "After so much time spent in painful *labour*, to arrive at once at the summit of my *desires*, was the most gratifying *consummation* of my toils" (p. 52; my italics). The sexual implications of the words emphasized are self-evident and surely intentional. To the extent that creativity calls for isolation and self-absorption, it might be regarded as a perversion of sexuality, specifically a form of masturbation or incest.[1] When it comes to creating a monstrous mate, there are similar hints that sexual energies are being improperly channelled: "I had an insurmountable aversion to the idea of *engaging* myself in my loathsome task in my father's house, while in habits of familiar *intercourse* with those I loved" (p. 152; my italics). In *Frankenstein* the curse of sexual perversion is pervasive. For example, the image of Frankenstein pursuing mother "nature to

47

her hiding places" has overtones both incestuous and necrophiliac: "I collected bones from charnel-houses; and disturbed, with profane fingers, the tremendous secrets of the human frame" (pp. 54-55). Such obsessions cannot be adequately explained in terms of a gothic convention.

Imagistically, Frankenstein's ambitions amount to a desire to sexually possess his dead mother. Following the successful animation of his monster, Frankenstein takes to his bed (an unlikely sequence on any literal level, as Irving Massey observes[2]) and experiences his Freudian fantasy in a dream. Much like the allegorical conflict in *Dr. Faustus* between the Good and Bad Angels, Frankenstein is presented with a choice between the healthy extroverted sexuality held out to him by his fiancée Elizabeth and that diseased, introverted, monstrous sexual passion he feels for his mother:

> I thought I saw Elizabeth, in the bloom of health, walking in the streets of Ingolstadt. Delighted and surprised, I embraced her; but as I imprinted the first kiss on her lips, they became livid with the hue of death; her features appeared to change, and I thought that I held the corpse of my dead mother in my arms; a shroud enveloped her form, and I saw the grave-worms crawling in the folds of the flannel. I started from my sleep with horror; a cold dew covered by forehead, my teeth chattered, and every limb became convulsed: when, by the dim and yellow light of the moon, as it forced its way through the window shutters, I beheld the wretch—the miserable monster whom I created. (p. 58)

Frankenstein's unnatural creation is introduced as a consequence of that unnatural passion that causes Elizabeth to metamorphose into his mother's corpse. The train of associations here suggests a pun, whether conscious or not, in the next paragraph where a comparison is made with "A mummy again endued with animation ..." (p. 58).

In the original version of *Frankenstein*, Elizabeth is less clearly opposed to the mother as a positive image of sexuality. Since she is there the daughter of Frankenstein's father's sister, Frankenstein's relationship with her is only some degrees less consanguineous than his relationship with his mother. However, one of the lengthier revisions in the 1831 version presents Elizabeth as related to the Frankenstein family only by adoption. Thus, and this I would deem a thematic improvement, a relatively clear opposition is initially established between destructive incest and true love. Subsequently, like other oppositions in the book, this one loses its apparent clarity.

While in the second edition most of the references to Elizabeth as "cousin" are routinely changed to "friend," "girl" or "Elizabeth" this does not always happen. In fact, increasingly, the term "cousin" is allowed to stand and imply a brother/sister element in the relationship that she and Frankenstein turn into that of husband and wife. Addressing Victor and Elizabeth from her death-bed as "My children," their mother had continued, "my firmest hopes of future happiness were placed on the prospect of your union" (p. 43). Later Frankenstein's father speaks to his son about his unquestionably ambiguous attitude towards Elizabeth. "You perhaps regard her as a sister, without any wish that she might become your wife. Nay, you may have met with another whom you may love; and considering yourself as bound in honour to Elizabeth, this struggle may occasion the poignant misery which you appear to feel." Frankenstein denies the charge but in echoing his mother's dying wish—"My future hopes and prospects are entirely bound up in the expectation of our union" (p. 151)—the spectre of Elizabeth's rival *is* invoked. In general terms, the spectre of incest is raised by Mary Shelley to suggest concerns which are enclosed, inturned and reflexive. Are we to intuit that the only love possible is that of Narcissus? If so what else in our environment is essentially a self-reflection? These are the questions that *Frankenstein* poses.

Other characters in the novel appear to be related in ways that amplify the motif of incest and perverted sexuality into a general condition. Following the murder of William, Frankenstein's younger brother, Clerval, Frankenstein's friend, intones: "dear lovely child, he now sleeps with his angel mother!" (p. 73). The exclamation mark at least allows for the possibility that some *double entendre* is being hinted at. Walton, the letter-writer of the outer narrative frame and the putative transcriber of the entire account, appears to enjoy an affectionate relationship with his sister Margaret. Since Walton's role largely mirrors Frankenstein's, it seems logical to impute an analogous incestuous attraction between the explorer and his "beloved Sister" (p. 212).

We have recently become attuned to the fact that literary works, to a greater or lesser degree, create roles for their readers.[3] In the case of *Frankenstein*, the reader is required to put himself in the role of Margaret. Walton has prepared the narrative specifically for her eyes. By means of this narrative strategy, the reader is drawn into a construct of reflecting mirrors and forced to identify with what may be seen as the injured party. As Robert Kiely points out, Frankenstein usurps not only the power of God but also the power of woman.[4] He discovers a means of creating life which avoids the sexual means of procreation. The female function is distorted not only by the inturning motif of incest but also by the more radically solipsistic alternatives of homosexuality and masturbation.

The relationship between Frankenstein and his best friend Clerval is not exactly homosexual but Clerval does come across as a rather feminine character. Thus the qualities that attract Frankenstein to Elizabeth find their reflection in Clerval: "he might not have been so perfectly humane, so thoughtful in his generosity—so full of kindness and tenderness amidst his passion for adventurous exploit, had she not unfolded to him the real loveliness of beneficence and made the doing good, the end and aim of his soaring ambition" (p. 38). On the eve of Frankenstein's departure for university, his relationship with Clerval seems more passionate than friendly: "We sat late. We could not tear ourselves away from each other ..." (p. 44). When Frankenstein becomes ill Clerval nurses him: "He [Clerval] knew that I could not have a more kind and attentive nurse than himself" (p. 62).

One should be careful not to oversimplify. The relationship with Clerval appears to hold both the alternative possibilities of homosexuality and ideal friendship. In this respect his role reflects the negative and positive aspects of Elizabeth's and poses a similar question. If all love is incestuous, is all friendship in *Frankenstein* homosexual? The sexual nature of Frankenstein's feelings for Clerval is alluded to in this passage describing his revived spirits:

> Study had before secluded me from the intercourse of my fellow creatures, and rendered me unsocial; but Clerval called forth the better feelings of my heart; he again taught me to love the aspect of nature, and the cheerful faces of children. Excellent friend! How sincerely did you love me and endeavour to elevate my mind until it was on a level with your own! A selfish pursuit had cramped and narrowed me until your gentleness and affection warmed and opened my senses ... (p. 70)

If further evidence is required of Clerval's femininity there is the likelihood, as I have indicated in Chapter 1, that his name derives from that of Claire Clairmont. Mary has simply exchanged the French words "val" and "mont." The more feminine valley replaces the masculine mountain.

A link is established between Frankenstein's latent homosexuality and his scientific interests through Waldman, by far the more congenial of the two professors who influence him at university. He is described in terms which suggest a mixture of masculine and feminine traits: "His person was short, but remarkably erect; and his voice the sweetest I had ever heard." It is this hermaphroditical gentleman who speaks, as Frankenstein is to speak, of the need to "penetrate into the recesses of nature, and show how she works in her hiding places" (p. 47).

The ambivalent sexuality of Frankenstein's various relationships implies as much about relationships generally as it does about Frankenstein himself. And this ambivalence assumes a stark reality in the imperfect being that Frankenstein creates. Ironically, having removed himself from the sphere of domestic affection, he creates a being who craves companionship and a wife.

Frankenstein's own impending marriage counterpoints and mocks the monster's desire for a mate. Repeatedly rebuffed, the monster comes to see that if he is to enjoy any kind of relationship it must be with someone who offers a reflection of himself: "I am alone, and miserable; man will not associate with me; but one as deformed and horrible as myself would not deny herself to me" (p. 144). He charges Frankenstein with making such a being and explains that his murderous career results from a denial of affection: "My vices are the children of a forced solitude ..." (p. 147). It was, of course, Frankenstein's enforced solitude that resulted in the begetting of the monster and, in murdering Frankenstein's friends and loved ones, the monster is essentially making manifest the consequences of that initial withdrawal.

A desire for friendship is initially voiced by Walton. In his second letter he writes: "But I have one want which I have never yet been able to satisfy; and the absence of the object of which I now feel as a most severe evil. I have no friend, Margaret." The friend for which he yearns, someone "gentle yet courageous, possessed of a cultivated as well as a capacious mind, whose tastes are like my own" (p. 19), is, of course, Frankenstein, who appears shortly, stranded on an ice floe. Frankenstein's reciprocal appreciation of Walton has an almost sexual quality causing Walton to record how "his lustrous eyes dwell on me with all their melancholy sweetness" (p. 31). Once again, the relationship desired and the relationship experienced is that of like for like. What is involved is not so much true feeling for another as self-love. But at the end of the book Walton is dissuaded from continuing his possibly suicidal and alienating quest for the North Pole in favour of returning to England and human community: "I may there find consolation" (p. 218). The question remains is there a real choice? The book's final impression is one of unrelieved loneliness. For a brief moment the three isolates, Walton, Frankenstein and the monster, are together in the same room. However, Frankenstein is dead, the monster projects his self-immolation and soon Walton is left entirely alone.[5]

An ambiguous statement by the monster crystallizes the problem. He has been reading *The Sorrows of Werther* while eavesdropping on the lives of a family of poor cottage dwellers: "The gentle and domestic manners it described, combined with lofty sentiments and feelings, which had for their object something out of self, accorded well with my experience among my protectors, and with the wants which were forever alive in my own bosom" (p. 128). The ambiguous phrase is, of course, "something out of self." A reader's first reaction would be to gloss the phrase as "something other than the self." But Mary did not write "something other than the self." What she actually wrote has a quite other additional meaning. It might be more directly

51

glossed as "something which comes out of the self." Love, as the relationships in *Frankenstein* appear to indicate, may be self-reflexive. I believe that the ambiguity here is deliberate, goes to the heart of the meaning of *Frankenstein* and is not to be resolved. Likewise is the case of the monster's later paradoxical apostrophe following his creator's death: "Oh Frankenstein! Generous and self-devoted being!" (p. 219). The contradictory qualities of generosity and self-love are presented as virtual synonyms.

The five interpolated stories variously probe the issues raised by the over-all thematic pattern of egotistic perversion, friendship and human relationships. In the first such insert, Walton describes the master of his ship, "a mariner equally noted for his kindness of heart and the respect and obedience paid to him by his crew." This man, "having amassed a considerable sum in prize-money," had been engaged to marry a Russian lady whom he loved. However, she loved another, a poor man whom her father regards as beyond the pale in terms of marriage. Straightway, the sailor made over his wealth to his rival and left the country not returning until his former mistress and her lover were married. Is this the yardstick of selflessness by which events in *Frankenstein* should be measured? Is this mariner Mary Shelley's equivalent of Swift's Portuguese sailor in *Gulliver's Travels*? Walton's account continues: " 'What a noble fellow!' you will exclaim. He is so; but then he is wholly uneducated: he is as silent as a Turk, and a kind of ignorant carelessness attends him, which, while it renders his conduct the more astonishing, detracts from the interest and sympathy which otherwise he would command" (p. 21). The monster is initially a similar prototype, a noble savage capable of intense feeling, but the account of the mariner clearly indicates that some modicum of intellectual accomplishment is a necessary part of human interaction. "[T]he interest and sympathy" the mariner presently fails to elicit is symptomatic of the love he failed to kindle in the heart of the Russian lady. Love and intellect may conflict but again they may not.

A second interpolation describes the circumstances of Frankenstein's father's marriage. His father's "most intimate" (p. 31) friend, Beaufort, a merchant, had fallen upon hard times and left Geneva with his daughter Caroline. When Frankenstein's father finally locates them, he finds Caroline in a distressed state after nursing Beaufort through a long illness from which he has just died. Two years later, Frankenstein's father married Caroline. Their love is rendered equivocal by the imagistic hint of incest. It is emphasized that, at the time, Frankenstein's father was already advanced in years. In marrying the daughter of a friend, he is marrying someone young enough to be his own daughter. Subsequently, Frankenstein draws attention to a picture of Caroline that combines possibilities of incest and necrophilia: "It was a historical subject, painted at my father's desire, and represented Caroline Beaufort in an agony of despair, kneeling by the coffin of her dead father" (p. 78).

The third interpolation concerns the introduction of Elizabeth to the family and sets up the ambiguous nature of her relationship with Frankenstein. As I have indicated, the version of this history in the 1831 edition constitutes a major revision of the 1818 version. In the earlier version, Elizabeth is Frankenstein's father's sister's daughter but in the lengthier revision she is not related. In the revision, Frankenstein's mother comes across Elizabeth while visiting the cottages of the poor near Lake Como. Elizabeth is one of a family of five children but, unlike the other four, she is thin and fair, "a distinct species, a being heaven-sent, and bearing a celestial stamp in all her features" (p. 34). The peasant mother explains that Elizabeth is not her child "but the daughter of a Milanese nobleman" (p. 35). Her German mother died on giving birth and Elizabeth was placed with this particular peasant family to be nursed. Following the death of her idealistic father, Elizabeth remained with her foster parents. Smitten, Frankenstein's mother arranges to adopt Elizabeth. As for Frankenstein's reaction, "We called each other familiarly by the name of cousin. No word, no expression could body forth the kind of relation in which she stood to me—my more than sister, since till death she was to be mine only" (p. 36). The intimations of immortality that she trails with her suggest a strong imagistic connection with Frankenstein's later metaphysical explorations. Like the monster, she appears to be "of a distinct species" (p. 34). To what extent, it must be asked, is Frankenstein's attachment to her contributive rather than opposed to the creation of his monster?

When Frankenstein's brother William is murdered, the family maid, Justine Moritz, is accused. Justine is rather awkwardly introduced, shortly before the discovery of William's body, in a fourth interpolation, this one in the context of a letter from Elizabeth to Frankenstein: "Do you remember on what occasion Justine Moritz entered our family? Probably you do not; I will relate her history, therefore, in a few words" (p. 64). Of itself, this ploy is a bit strained but the sense of dislocation is augmented by the information that she was a member of the household when Frankenstein was there, and present at his mother's death. She might have been referred to then rather than just before her presence becomes dramatically necessary. It is "flaws" such as this (perhaps deliberately contrived) that make the book, like the monster, seem something of a botched job. The same applies to the interpolations themselves; they suggest a patchwork effect. However, at the same time they are consistent with the enveloping patchwork structure of the entire narrative. The monster's story is inserted within Frankenstein's which, in turn, is inserted within Walton's communications to his sister.

Justine's story details the consequences of withheld affection. She was the disliked third child of a widow with four children. On seeing the situation, Frankenstein's mother had persuaded the widow to let her take in Justine, then aged twelve, as a servant. Justine formed a strong attachment to Frankenstein's mother and became ill following her death. Subsequently, her own brothers and sister died, leaving her mother isolated and feeling guilty about her neglected surviving daughter. Justine returned home at her mother's request. Their relationship was not altogether improved. Madame Mortiz reverted to blaming Justine rather than herself for her misfortunes. However, Justine fulfilled her family obligations and remained at home until her mother's death "on the first approach of cold weather" (p. 66), whereupon Justine returned to the Frankenstein residence. Elizabeth notes that Justine's admiration for Frankenstein's mother led her "to imitate her phraseology and manners, so that even now she often reminds me of her" (p. 65). Elizabeth ends her account by referring again to this similarity and thus further emphasizing the extent to which a loving relationship depends upon or encourages a solipsistic likeness.

It is the monster's unlikeness that repeatedly frustrates his efforts at human contact. He gains an awareness of everything from which he is excluded during the period of education when he eavesdrops on a humble, affectionate family who live in a cottage. The arrival of Safie, the Arabian with whom the son Felix is in love, provides the monster with a somewhat contrived opportunity to benefit from her English lessons and, in the process, discover something about the complexities of human relationships. What the monster learns about Safie and her relationship with Felix forms the substance of the fifth, final and most extended interpolation accounting for the whole of Chapter 14. It is the book's central narrative unit.

The monster recounts how the poor cottagers, De Lacey, his son, ironically named Felix—"the saddest of the group" (p. 113)—and his daughter Agatha, had in more prosperous days lived in Paris. Also in Paris at that time was Safie's father, a Turkish merchant, who was, it seems, unjustly thrown in jail to await execution. It is at this point that the repeated motif of unjust trials connects with the successive interpolated accounts of human relationships. Felix, present at the trial, vows to engineer the Turk's escape. On visiting the Turk, he meets and falls in love with another visitor, the daughter Safie. To secure Felix's help, the Turk holds out the prospect of marriage to Safie. With the help of a translator, Safie writes Felix letters in French in which she describes how her Christian mother was captured and made a slave of the Turks, one of whom married her. Safie explains that her hopes of marrying a Christian and living an emancipated life derive from her mother. The information in Safie's letters amounts to an interpolation within an interpolation which may be seen as the innermost structural and, if Rubenstein is correct, psycho-biographical core of the narrative.

Thanks to Felix's help, the Turk escapes from prison the day before his expected execution and joins Felix and Safie in Italy to await a favourable opportunity to return to Turkey. He also awaits an opportunity to separate Safie from Felix since the idea of his daughter marrying a Christian is, in fact, abhorrent to him. Events favour the Turk's double-crossing intent. The French government, having discovered that Felix was responsible for the escape of their prisoner, throw his father and sister in jail. Felix returns to Paris and stands trial. The result of this trial—unjust by any human standards —is that the De Laceys are deprived of their wealth and exiled. While the De Laceys finally settle in the cottage in Germany where the monster comes across them, the Turk seizes the chance to flee to Constantinople with the idea that his daughter should follow. Instead, Safie seeks out Felix.

This prolonged account of true love and treachery bears more directly on the situation of the monster and Frankenstein than do the other interpolations. Safie in Germany, "alone, unacquainted with the language of the country, and utterly ignorant of the customs of the world" (p. 127), shares something of the monster's plight. The love she and Felix feel for one another is as genuine as the monster's collective love for the De Laceys. And just as the Turk acts treacherously towards Felix and Safie, so Frankenstein acts treacherously in failing to take responsibility for the well-being of his creation.

As nowhere else in the novel, the opposition between what appears positive —true love—and what appears negative—treachery—seems absolute. But Safie's attraction to Felix is based primarily on the element of likeness—he is a Christian—and the Turk's shabby intentions have to do with a lack of likeness—Felix is not a follower of Muhammed. Owing to her mother's influence, Safie had contemplated abandoning her birthplace and, in effect, denying her patrimony. And it should not be forgotten that the precipitating action of this interpolated history—the Turk's being thrown in jail—may be considered an act of treachery of which the Turk is the victim, not the perpetrator. The monster notes simply that the Turk's presence in Paris "became obnoxious to the government" "for some reason I could not learn." The logic of the history and of *Frankenstein* generally implies that what was at fault was simply the Turk's unlikeness. Indeed, "it was judged that his religion and wealth, rather than the crime alleged against him, had been the cause of his condemnation" (p. 122). At this point, the monster's own "obnoxious" unlikeness suggests an affinity with the Turk rather than with Safie. But this inextricable involvement of opposites is manifest in Safie's own person. Because of her mixed parentage, she is both Turkish and Arabian, Muhammadan and Christian. She epitomizes that thematic material in *Frankenstein* which organizes itself not so much in terms of egotistic perversion *or* domestic affection but rather egotistic perversion *and* domestic affection. The one thing appears to be the same as the other.

(ii)   *The Doppelgänger Theme*

In considering the literary sources of *Frankenstein*, I alluded to the tradition of the doppelgänger.[6] However, this tradition is not a source in the specific sense that the other literary sources provided Mary with various spare parts. The doppelgänger motif constitutes an aspect of the book's thematic design and may not profitably be traced to any particular text or texts. *Frankenstein* simply takes its place in a literary tradition, the durability of which owes something to the nature of literature itself. To the extent that a writer peoples his pages with the creations of his own brain, his various characters may be regarded as alter egos. But the doppelgänger is most naturally suited to allegorical treatment as in the case of the medieval psychomachia. Although *Frankenstein* is far from being an overt allegory, there appears to be a growing consensus amongst critics that, from a certain point of view, the monster should be regarded as Frankenstein's double, "something out of self" (p. 128) in the monster's phrase. This insight was first directly recorded by Muriel Spark in 1951 and subsequently variously amplified by others.[7] A number of recent commentators, however, have denied the existence of any doppelgänger connection. Burton R. Pollin, for example, notes that Spark's *Child of Light* "offers the thesis—untenable in my eyes—that the monster constitutes Frankenstein's *Doppelgänger*."[8]

The problem, of course, is that Spark's interpretation makes manifest an allegorical dimension in a book the overriding tone of which is realistic. All manner of interpretative difficulties follow. If the monster is some kind of psychological projection, what of the other characters who either interact with him or are physically affected by his presence? Must they also be understood as aspects of Frankenstein's personality?[9] The answer, I believe, is both yes and no. The epistemological assumptions of realism coexist with the contradictory assumptions of allegory. The monster is both a psychological double and an independent character leading a realistic existence.

This dilemma exists in the context of the relationship between egotistic perversion and communal affection. From one point of view, the monster is different from Frankenstein, from another, he is the same person. From one point of view, egotistic perversion is very different from communal affection, from another, it amounts to the same thing. As my discussion has indicated, successful relationships with others in *Frankenstein* seem suspiciously close to relationships with mirror images, with doubles. At one point, Frankenstein observes that "in Clerval I saw the image of my former self" (p. 158). I avoided using the word "double" or "doppelgänger" in that previous section but the notion is clearly implicit in the affection/perversion business and, indeed, what I have distinguished as two thematic configurations should be regarded as one.

In this light, it is possible at least directly to face up to, if not exactly answer, the difficult question that most interpreters of the book have either sidestepped or simplified—exactly what aspect of Frankenstein does the monster represent? The usual conclusion, that the monster represents the destructive and diabolical nature of Frankenstein's overweaning intellectual ambition does not square with the actual presentation of the monster as a noble savage, an innocent more sinned against than sinning. What we have to do with here is a false splitting of the apparently good and the apparently evil. In a world where the concept of love is rendered ambiguously akin to incest, homosexuality and masturbation by the human tendency to transform the other into a replica of the self, the monster is, it would seem, that unalterable Other, and therefore the potential source and object of genuine love. But, at the same time, if human love is truly a matter of incest, homosexuality and masturbation then the monster represents the self that Frankenstein—and the reader—do not wish to recognize.

The ambiguities stated here in terms of love should also be understood in terms of the pursuit of scientific knowledge. Frankenstein's obsession with the secret of life cuts him off from the lives of friends and relations; does it also cut him off from an awareness of the possibility that what he takes to be the otherness of the life or reality that he is studying may be within himself? As with love, what appears to be outer directed may be egotistically inner directed. Both the nature of love and the nature of knowledge appear to be ambiguously self-reflective. The denial of this self-reflective element leads to the kind of schizophrenia evident in the relationship between Frankenstein and the monster. But this may not be the case and, thus again, the monster— the Other—is real. No one alternative should be chosen. Mary is dealing with the philosophical mysteries raised by all relationships between an I and an Other.

All of this paradoxical profundity will, of course, have no real bearing unless the reader of *Frankenstein* picks up the clues that establish the doppelgänger connection. And since, as I have indicated, some scholars have recently denied this connection, it may be worthwhile to trace the relevant evidence. A careful reader coming to the book, as surely virtually every reader does, with some knowledge of the basic plot idea may observe some calculation in Mary's early use of the words "animation" and "animated" in relation to Frankenstein. Frankenstein is near death when he boards Walton's ship: "as soon as he had quitted the fresh air, he fainted. We ... restored him to animation by rubbing him with brandy, and forcing him to swallow a small quantity" (p. 25). After hearing that Walton had previously observed the being that Frankenstein is pursuing, "a new spirit of life animated the decaying frame of the stranger." If this is not quite the same as the animation of Frankenstein's creation, it is certainly presented as a kind of resurrection. Frankenstein himself admits, "you have benevolently restored me to life" (p. 26).

By applying to Frankenstein the words "animation" and "animated" which also point to this monster, the result of his capability of "bestowing animation upon lifeless matter" (p. 52), Mary is implying an identity between the creator and his creation. Just before Frankenstein begins his narrative, Walton provides a retrospective image of the man with "his thin hand raised in animation, while the lineaments of his face are irradiated by the soul within" (p. 31). There is an element of tautology in this description which is worth stressing. It is Frankenstein's soul, spirit or anima that maintains his carcass in a state of animation. The relationship here between "soul" and "animation" suggests, as I shall subsequently argue in detail, that Frankenstein's ambitions are of a religious nature. However, at present it is only necessary to note that in the brief number of pages given to Walton's initial view of Frankenstein the word "animation" is used twice and the word "animated" once. To any reader aware of what is to come, the effect is to trigger an association between Frankenstein and the monster.

In fact, wherever someone is presented as being "animated" an attentive reader will think of the monster. There is no logical reason to limit the range of doppelgänger relationships. If the monster is actually some kind of psychological projection, who else or what else should be viewed similarly? Perhaps everybody if not everything. Following the death of Justine and with a sharpened sense of the fallen state of the world, Elizabeth claims that "men appear to me as monsters thirsting for each other's blood" (p. 92). I have already referred to the sense that Frankenstein and Walton, like Justine and Frankenstein's mother, are doubles. If the word "animated" is leant on in the way I suggest it should be, this doubling tendency multiplies. Frankenstein's par-

58

ents, Clerval and Elizabeth all become hypothetical doubles of the monster or Frankenstein. Frankenstein speaks of his parents' conscientiousness towards himself as a child, "the being to which they had given life" and "the active spirit of tenderness that animated both" (p. 34) of them. Elizabeth's eyes "were ever there to bless and animate us" (p. 38). Clerval both benefits from these eyes and himself possesses an "animated glance" (p. 44). Subsequently, it is the monster who assumes the Frankenstein role when he rescues a drowning girl and attempts to "restore animation" (p. 141).

This last example brings us back to that narrower correspondence, the careful process whereby the reader comes to suspect that the name Frankenstein may apply to both the creator and his creation.[10] After all, in different ways either Frankenstein or his monster might be regarded as *The Modern Prometheus* of the subtitle. While Frankenstein mimics Prometheus' role as the creator of man, the monster rebels against his creator much as Prometheus rebelled against Zeus.[11] And as I have indicated in the previous chapter, it appears from the Miltonic analogies that both Frankenstein and the monster are akin to Adam and Satan.

There is real basis in the text for believing that the monster is Frankenstein in both name and substance. The fact that the creation and escape of the monster is barely described and, indeed, is deliberately denied the kind of empirical reality conveyed in cinematic adaptations, leaves the essential nature of the being open. The monster's first live entrance is presented as a consequence of Frankenstein's dream. Such circumstances certainly augment the sense that the monster is some kind of psychological projection and may even hint that much of the narrative is a dream or an hallucination—were it not, perhaps, for Walton's "framing" account. It should be further observed that the monster is introduced and takes his leave hovering over a prone Frankenstein; in the first case, Frankenstein is asleep in his bed, in the second, he is dead in his coffin; in the first case, Frankenstein (on "awakening") thinks of "A mummy again endued with animation" (p. 58), in the second, Walton (who, like Frankenstein earlier, is appreciating the horror of the creature for the first time) relates the texture and colour of the monster's "vast hand" to "that of a mummy" (p. 218).

This business of the monster hovering over Frankenstein is one of three occasions in the text where the elements of one scene are metamorphically reproduced in another. The situation where the scenery of Switzerland and the scenery of Germany come together was treated in the last chapter; the third case will be treated in the next. In general terms this reduplicative metamorphosis is a technical means of signalling the possibility that elements which appear to be distinct, separate and self-contained, may actually constitute an indivisible unity.

In the present case, it might be argued more specifically that the second tableau of the monster hanging over the horizontal figure of his creator makes manifest what is only metaphorical in the first tableau. If the life which Frankenstein bestows upon the monster is actually his own and the relationship between the differing qualities or natures they represent is antagonistic rather than symbiotic, then the animation of the one should bring about the inanimation or death of the other. The paradoxical terminology in Frankenstein's statement, "I conceived the idea, and executed the creation of a man" (p. 211), might be taken as expressing this involvement of life and death. And, in fact, following the monster's vivication, Frankenstein reveals, "I was lifeless and did not recover my senses for a long, long time." Were it not for the ministrations of his friend Clerval, "nothing ... could have restored me to life" (p. 62). Frankenstein is as much a Lazurus as his monster and twice the power of friendship, exercised first by Clerval and secondly by Walton, in the frozen Arctic wastes, brings about his resurrection. In retrospect, Frankenstein sees that he has been involved in a life-death struggle with this creation. The words of Professor Waldman, which initially inspired Frankenstein, were fatalistically "enounced to destroy me. As he went on, I felt as if my soul were grappling with a palpable enemy" (p. 48).

Soon after coming into contact with Frankenstein, Walton senses that "the man has a double existence: he may suffer misery, and be overwhelmed by disappointments; yet when he has retired into himself, he will be like a celestial spirit, that has a halo around him, within whose circle no grief or folly ventures" (p. 29). The monster is that celestial spirit. When he is not called a monster, a creature, a wretch, a fiend or a thing, he is referred to as a daemon (e.g., pp. 26, 76, 85, 165, 166, 203, 204, 219), a word which has been corrupted into demon but which originally meant simply spirit, whether good or bad.[12] It is Frankenstein himself who suggests that the monster be identified as his evil spirit: "I considered the being whom I had cast among mankind, and endowed with the will and power to effect purposes of horror ... nearly in the light of my own vampire, my own spirit let loose from the grave, and forced to destroy all that was dear to me" (p. 77). The monster is Jekyll to Frankenstein's Hyde. Or is it the reverse?

Following the death of William and the execution of Justine, Frankenstein "wandered like an evil spirit" (p. 90). Although Justine, persuaded for a while by her confession that she did actually kill young William, says, "I almost began to think that I was the monster that he [her confessor] said I was" (p. 87), the full force of this metaphorical recognition is reserved for Frankenstein as the creator of the *actual* monster who did murder William and caused Justine to be unjustly executed. The daemon is now clearly a demon, a fiend: "My abhorrence of this fiend cannot be conceived. When I thought of him, I gnashed my teeth, my eyes became inflamed, and I ardently wished to extinguish that life which I had so thoughtlessly bestowed" (p. 92). This expression of hatred puts Frankenstein in the monster role. He looks to Elizabeth "to chase away the fiend that lurked in my heart" (p. 93). But ultimately, Frankenstein sees himself as responsible for Elizabeth's death: "I am the cause of this—I murdered her. William, Justine, and Henry—they all died by my hands" (p. 185). "I am the assassin of those most innocent creatures; they died by my machinations" (p. 186).

I have no wish to transform likely defects into artistic virtues but, given this process of self-recognition, it is at least possible to argue that Frankenstein's failure to register surprise on first discovering that his creation can speak English is appropriate and revelatory since he is, in fact, speaking to himself. However this may be, as the narrative progresses, Mary makes increasing use of various kinds of reversals to further indicate that Frankenstein and the monster are ambiguously differentiated aspects of a single being. Although for the monster Frankenstein is equivalent to God, Frankenstein finds himself in a position where he must accede to his creation's wishes and manufacture a mate. "But," claims Frankenstein, "through the whole period during which I was the slave of my creature, I allowed myself to be governed by the impulses of the moment" (p. 153). This kind of ambiguous appositional syntax is frequently employed to reflect the book's thematic ambiguities. Here the question arises, is Frankenstein the "slave" of his inner "impulses" or is he "governed" by his "creature?" Once again, the distinction between what is external and what is internal is being conflated. According to the daemon's own account of his resolve to kill Elizabeth, "I was the slave, not the master, of an impulse, which I detested, yet could not disobey." After the death of Elizabeth, the monster declares with Milton's Satan[13] that "Evil thenceforth became my good" (p. 220). But in Mary Shelley's context, the phrase carries the implication that evil and good are in a sense synonymous.

On at least a couple of occasions a different kind of ironic reversal takes place when Frankenstein attributes to the monster qualities which might more appropriately be attributed to Frankenstein himself. While engaged in creating a mate, as agreed, Frankenstein observes the monster at his laboratory window: "As I looked on him, his countenance expressed the utmost extent of malice and treachery." Given that, in the next instant, Frankenstein

61

"tore to pieces the thing on which [he] was engaged" (p. 166), it is he and
not the monster who is guilty of treachery. He has gone back on his word. At
a later point, a dying Frankenstein attempts to convince Walton of the need
to destroy the monster: "He is eloquent and persuasive ... His soul is as
hellish as his form, full of treachery and fiendlike malice" (p. 209). Once
again, these qualities might more appropriately be applied to the man who
is so compellingly advocating murder.[14]

The inextricable interinvolvement of Frankenstein and the monster is conveyed most concretely in terms of the ambiguous reversal of pursuer and
pursued in the final quarter of the narrative. First it is the monster who
follows Frankenstein but, after the murder of Elizabeth, Frankenstein proceeds to track his creation. For a moment, Frankenstein recognizes that the
very creature he is tracking, fearing "that if I lost all trace of him I should
despair and die, left some mark to guide me." But immediately Frankenstein rejects this attribution of benevolence to the monster and imagines "a
spirit of good" which, in some paradoxical fashion, "followed and directed
my steps" (p. 203). As Frankenstein sees things, it is the spirit of good and
not the monster that places meals in his path.

If a reader is not ready at this point to entertain the possibility that Frankenstein and the monster are psychic doubles, further argumentation on my
part will make little difference. But a couple of additional points should be
made. The fact that one of Mary's best tales, "The Transformation" (1830),
is undisputedly about a doppelgänger relationship between a dissolute young
man and a misshapen dwarf who exchange identities does suggest that the
evidence for a similar relationship in *Frankenstein* should be viewed in a
positive light.[15] However, as a final piece of internal evidence we return to
the monster's references to the "series of my being" (pp. 219, 222). I have
already made the point that amongst the meanings that might be derived
from this teasing phrase is the idea that the monster is co-existent with the
series of incidents that make up the text itself. But the word "series" also
serves as a point of identification with Frankenstein who earlier speaks of
the "whole series of my life" (p. 178). In a sense, then, Frankenstein, the
monster and the text constitute an identical reality. And what, after all, is a
series but a sequence of separate yet connected elements moving towards
wholeness or oneness?

By now it should be readily apparent that the doppelgänger theme and
the thematic emphasis on patterns of sexual perversion—especially incest
and homosexuality—are aspects of one another. If the relationship between
Frankenstein and his monster is symptomatic of the self-reflective nature of

all relationships then all relationships are self-involved. That self-involvement might forcibly be imaged as masturbatory but, given the exigencies of plot, what is actually masturbatory is presented more often as incestuous or homosexual. Irving Massey has realized that the monster's desire for a female mate is, in truth, only a pretext. The fact that "rape is the one crime he won't commit"[16]—even when presented with an unconscious Justine—suggests that his real desire is not directed towards women. Even allowing for the overt element of male chauvinism, there is truth in this remark. Frankenstein is clearly "the monster's only true love."[17] This love is finally acknowledged when the monster describes the dead Frankenstein as "the select specimen of all that is worthy of love and admiration among men" (p. 222).

So far I have explained the doppelgänger relationship as if Frankenstein were a representative man. His schizophrenia reflects the morally ambiguous nature of love and knowledge in our "fallen" world. But the book's impact depends upon the reader's intuition that while from one point of view, the mind of Frankenstein constitutes the entire narrative reality, from another, he is but a man among men. Between the extreme subjective and the extreme objective positions, the reader is faced with an infinity of choices as to what elements of seemingly external reality are to be understood as projections of Frankenstein's psyche. At one point on this spectrum the monster is as real as everybody else, at least as literal as the bug in Kafka's *The Metamorphosis*. After all, to Walton's perception the monster does survive Frankenstein's death. If, however, carefully sifting the evidence, the reader attempts to square the narrative with everyday reality and rest for a while with the notion that the monster is a projection of Frankenstein but most everything else is real, then some psychological explanation must be found for the pattern of murders, Frankenstein's apparent desire to murder those nearest and dearest to him. He presumably does not kill Clerval and Elizabeth for philosophical and epistemological reasons. Such reasons will only do if Clerval and Elizabeth are somehow aspects of Frankenstein's reality.

Given that the world of Frankenstein is basically familial, what is required on the level of psychological realism is some kind of proto-Freudian motivation. Mary Shelley has been careful to include the necessary evidence but, as is wise in such matters, she avoids drawing explicit conclusions. The reader should, however, understand Frankenstein's psychology as distinct from the kind of intimations, described in Chapter 2, that might be gleaned from the novel concerning Mary Shelley's own psychology. We have seen that the creation of the monster is intimately related to the dream in which Frankenstein embraces his mother's corpse. His mother died of scarlet fever. Elizabeth, who previously contracted the disease and recovered, was the source of the contagion. Consequently, as Martin Tropp astutely hypothesizes, at least subconsciously, Frankenstein must blame Elizabeth for causing his mother's death.[18] This would explain the necessity for Elizabeth's death and—although Tropp does not make the point—the death of Clerval since he shares many of Elizabeth's qualities. (Tropp rationalizes the death of Clerval somewhat differently as the destruction of Frankenstein's moral side.[19]) As Frankenstein's doppelgänger, the monster shares his love for his mother; hence it is the miniature of Frankenstein's mother which William is carrying that "softened and attracted" (p. 143) the monster. Tropp further supposes that Frankenstein would have subconsciously resented Elizabeth for ending his idyllic life as an only child.[20] Hence again, the death of Elizabeth and the deaths of William and Justine. Nor is it accidental that the biographical situation of Justine herself, described in the chapter following Frankenstein's dream, presents, as Tropp observes, an analogous case.[21] Her mother "accused her of having caused the death of her brothers and sister" (p. 66), presumably out of suppressed hatred.

If we follow Tropp's argument that Victor subconsciously wants to destroy all the rivals for his parents' love, we are provided with a possible explanation for the survival of his father—the only member of the household not killed directly by the monster (he dies "naturally" of grief). In view of the evidence concerning Frankenstein's intense feelings for his mother, we must assume a pronounced ambivalence in his feelings for his father. Something of the love/hate relationship between Frankenstein and his monster also exists between father and son here. We may intuit, then, that Victor's father and the monster are not killed for analogous reasons. The Oedipal complexities inherent in Victor's attitude towards his father are hinted at during the period in Ireland following Clerval's murder. Frankenstein finds himself in prison as the suspected murderer; Mr. Kirwin, a magistrate, tells him that a friend is to visit. Frankenstein's reaction is one of horror: "I know not by what chain of thought the idea presented itself, but it instantly darted into my mind that the murderer had come to mock at my misery and taunt me with the death of Clerval, as a new incitement for me to comply with his hellish desires." Mr. Kirwin is bewildered: "I should have thought, young man, that the presence of your father would have been welcome, instead of inspiring such violent repugnance." Immediately, Frankenstein's reaction changes from "anguish to pleasure" (p. 180). What is here bewildering to Mr. Kirwin may be taken by the reader as revelatory of Frankenstein's psychology. The episode serves to identify Victor's father with the monster.

Little is to be gained by filling out and schematizing these psychological hints. It is enough to realize that events can be generally construed in a way that accords with Frankenstein's inner drives.[22] To turn the book into any kind of rigorous case history would be to inhibit that flexibility which enables the reader to move along the axis bounded at one end by Frankenstein as a man among men and at the other by Frankenstein as total reality. The interchangeable alignment of interior and exterior worlds, of psychology and mythology, allows for that metaphoric power which is at the heart of the book's vitality.

CHAPTER FOUR

"Spirit of Life":
Metaphoric Nexus

It is often said of characters in a successful novel that they "live" and "breathe." Works of art survive or die. The artist generally, and particularly the writer, has the Frankensteinian job of imbuing inert material with vitality. Of course, this kind of talk is metaphoric, not literal. But, it might be countered, what kind of talk is not metaphorical? There exists no agreed distinction between the literal and the metaphoric. Metaphor is often located as a major aspect of literary imagery. And imagery, associated with the imagination and the imaginary, is often thought of as having an antithetical relationship with the real. But this apparent distinction collapses as soon as it is allowed that our "picture" of reality derives from a totality of sensory images as codified by the human brain. The monster speaks of "the images which this world affords" (p. 222). Reality is a mysterious transactional compromise between what may be out there and what exists within the human skull.

Likewise, metaphor involves a conjunction of the internal and the external, of human and non-human factors. It is this assimilation of the non-human that makes all metaphor implicitly monstrous. This is all the more obvious, as Stanley Corngold argues, in the case of Kafka's *The Metamorphosis*, where a metaphor is in some sense literalized.[1] And *Frankenstein* is, in this respect, like *The Metamorphosis*. But it is this monstrous conjunction of the inner and outer that makes the mechanics of metaphor correspond to the mechanics of epistemology, the way in which we build up our knowledge of reality. Moreover, it should be emphasized that this is not just a matter of philosophy. The current state of post-Einsteinian science corroborates the philosophical suspicion that reality has a distinct shimmer. To the extent, then, that metaphor exhibits a fluid, shimmering quality, it conveys something of the quality of reality or life itself. And hence the long-standing critical notion that the essence of literature, especially poetry, is metaphor.

Consequently, in the case of *Frankenstein*, our search for that aspect of the book that makes it live so persistently and corresponds to the electrical charge that animates the monster, must result in an exploration of metaphoric

66

content. Unlike the thematic elements discussed in the previous chapter which proceed horizontally, metaphor radiates its meaning from a central core. In diagrammatic terms, its effect occurs concentrically or vertically. Accordingly, the elucidation of a book's metaphoric content will likely illuminate the essentially vertical nature of its "idea" or "ideas." The central metaphor or symbol (the distinction is basically a matter of metaphoric density and literalization) in *Frankenstein* is the monster himself. Starting with the proposition that the monster symbolizes the book, my concern throughout is with the complexities of that core symbol. For more reasons than one, therefore, it is appropriate that the monster's narrative forms the book's structural core, a core from which the narratives of Frankenstein and Walton may be viewed as radiating.

The overtly metaphoric content of *Frankenstein* derives from Mary's treatment of the forms and phenomena of the natural world. In particular, she focusses on those elements that might be construed as concretized states of mind or tokens of spiritual power, or both. The landscape, like the monster, partakes of human life. But life itself is associated with the realm of spirit and it is towards that realm that the more daunting aspects of the natural world appear to point. The Alpine and Arctic settings and the associated forces of magnetism, lightning and electricity are manifestations of transcendence. So much, of course, is implicit in the nature of metaphor. To speak metaphorically of the verticality of metaphor may, in fact, imply that its range is distributed between the upper sphere of Heaven and lower sphere of Hell.

(i)   *The Sublime Setting*

Of major relevance to an understanding of Mary's perception and description of landscape is an awarenes of eighteenth-century theories of the picturesque and the sublime. The difference is largely one of scale. A picturesque landscape reinforces human values and operates within human dimensions. A sublime landscape suggests a much enlarged order of reality. Descending the Rhine with Clerval below Mainz, where it "becomes much more picturesque" (p. 155), Frankenstein records an unexpected alternation of the sublime and the homely picturesque: "In one spot you view rugged hills, ruined castles overlooking tremendous precipices, with the dark Rhine rushing beneath; and on the sudden turn of a promontory, flourishing vineyards with green sloping banks and a meandering river and populous towns occupy the scene." For Clerval, the essentially picturesque nature of the German landscape is reassuring: "Oh, surely, the spirit that inhabits and guards this place

67

has a soul more in harmony with man, than those who pile the glacier or retire to the inaccessible peaks of the mountains of our own country" (p. 156).

But in *Frankenstein* the picturesque setting is infrequent and always something of a cheat. The sense of security it arouses or reflects is always short-lived and serves to set off something much less cosy. Chapter 6 ends with Frankenstein in an unusually buoyant mood: "A serene sky and verdant fields filled me with ecstacy. The present season was indeed divine; the flowers of spring bloomed in the hedges, while those of summer were already in bud" (p. 70). At the beginning of Chapter 7, Frankenstein learns that William has been murdered.

It is the sublime settings—the region around Mont Blanc and the Arctic wastelands—which predominate among the book's scenic effects. The history of the sublime as a philosophical category is lengthy and complicated. Of present concern is what may be termed the natural sublime as distinct from the earlier concept of a rhetorical sublime which consists of certain stylistic devices elaborated by Longinus. Marjorie Hope Nicolson provides an excellent account of the development of the natural sublime in *Mountain Gloom and Mountain Glory*.[2] She observes that while Longinus did regard the power of forming great conceptions as essential to the achievement of the sublime, it was not until the new astronomy and the new geology of the seventeenth century precipitated a new sense of the vastness of space and time that natural analogies were found for those sublime emotions previously associated directly with the deity. Mountains and oceans, once regarded as fallen disfigurements of the originally smooth surface of the mundane egg Earth, together with the reaches of interstellar space, were suddenly appreciated as evocative of the sublime emotions of terror and religious awe.

Thomas Burnet in his extraordinary *The Sacred Theory of the Earth* (1684) (a work which occupies a pivotal position in the aesthetic history of the sublime) touches on the three natural stimuli of the sublime in the following passage:

> The greatest Objects of Nature are, methinks, the most pleasing to behold; and next to the Great Concave of the Heavens, and those boundless regions where the Stars inhabit, there is nothing that I look upon with more Pleasure than the wide Sea and the Mountains of the Earth. There is something august and stately in the Air of these things, that inspires the Mind with great Thoughts and Passions; we do naturally, upon such Occasions, think of God and His greatness: And whatsoever hath but the Shadow and Appearance of INFINITE, as all things do have that are too big for our comprehension, they fill and overbear the Mind with their Excess, and cast it into a pleasing kind of Stupor and Admiration.[3]

Walton alludes to the same three "Objects" when he notes of Frankenstein that "The starry sky, the sea, and every sight afforded by these wonderful regions [the mountainous Arctic], seem still to have the power of elevating his soul from earth" (p. 29). Even the most casual reader of *Frankenstein* cannot fail to notice that a considerable portion of the book is given over to natural description, particularly of "the sublime shapes of the mountains" (p. 36) and tempestuous seas. The plot does not allow for any space voyages but that sublime region is at least implied by the repeated references to the moon. Robert M. Philmus undoubtedly speaks for many readers when he complains that the landscape in *Frankenstein* severely interrupts the development of the plot.[4] I hope to show that what Philmus regards as a negative feature is actually the source of the book's vitality. Towards this end it is important to appreciate that Mary Shelley chose to emphasize certain natural phenomena with an eye to evoking the natural sublime.

The qualities that constitute the sublime experience have been variously analysed. Joseph Addison in his *Pleasures of the Imagination* (1712) emphasizes the importance of the uncommon while Edmund Burke in *A Philosophical Enquiry into the Origin of our Ideas of the Sublime and Beautiful* (1757) stresses the value of obscurity because it excites fear of the unknown, specifically as related to the ideas of infinity and eternity. According to Burke, astonishment "is the effect of the sublime in its highest degree, but terror is the ruling principle of the sublime."[5] He claims that "the English *astonishment* and *amazement*, point out . . . clearly the kindred emotions which attend fear and wonder."[6] But it is an awareness of the power implied by sublime phenomena which produces the emotion of terror and that "delightful horror, which is the most genuine effect and truest test of the sublime."[7]

Clearly, the sublime experience offered in *Frankenstein* has much in common with Burke's prescription. It is the powerful and terrifying aspects of mountains and seas which make the strongest impression. As for the moon, while it is not overtly powerful or terrifying (except for the reader conscious of the moon's influence on the tide), it gains those qualities by being consistently associated with the monster. By a light half-dead, "the half-extinguished light" of a candle, Frankenstein first observes the process of animation: "I saw the dull yellow eye of the creature open; it breathed hard, and a convulsive motion agitated its limbs" (p. 57). Frankenstein, asleep after taking to his bed in horror, awakens to further horror: "my teeth chattered, and every limb became convulsed: when, by the dim and yellow light of the moon, as it forced its way through the window shutters, I beheld the wretch—the miserable monster whom I had created" (p. 58). The equation between the monster and the moon is doubly confirmed. "The dull yellow eye" of the one is complemented by "the dim yellow light" of the other. Because of a syntactical ambiguity, it is unclear whether the moon's light or the "wretch" "forced its way through the window shutters." It should also be observed that the "convulsive motion" which agitated the monster's limbs is transferred to Frankenstein whose "every limb became convulsed." Here is further evidence that the monster is Frankenstein's double. But since the moon and the monster are identified, should the moon also be seen as a projection of Frankenstein's inner reality? The answer, as should be apparent from my previous argumentation and as will become increasingly clear during the balance of this book, is both yes and no.

Amidst the confused sensations that characterize the monster's initial moments of awareness, he observes "a radiant form rise from among the trees." This, "the only object that I could distinguish was the bright moon," and by its light, like Caliban, with "innumerable sounds" (p. 103) ringing in his ears, the monster goes in search of berries. Much later, Frankenstein in his Orkneys laboratory "saw by the light of the moon, the daemon at the casement" (p. 166). Shortly thereafter, while "hung over" the body of Elizabeth (as the monster twice hangs over his own body), Frankenstein "felt a kind of panic on seeing the pale yellow light of the moon illuminate the chamber" (p. 196). Frankenstein's associative processes do not play him false. Once again the monster is at the window. When Frankenstein next sees the monster, having sworn vengeance and been disturbed by a familiar voice at his ear, the same association applies: "Suddenly the broad disk of the moon arose, and shone full upon his ghastly and distorted shape as he fled with more than mortal speed" (p. 203).

I have documented the connection between the moon and the monster in order to show how the qualities of Burke's sublime, most obviously manifested in Mary Shelley's descriptions of mountains and raging seas, are also attached to the moon. But the qualities which the monster bestows on the moon he himself appears to gain from the Alpine environment. The monster is almost a projection of the sensations inspired by the book's Alpine setting, the same setting which so affected Thomas Burnet and many of the other testifiers to mountain glory. The monster is at least as much a creation of the mountainous setting as of Frankenstein's more constrained laboratory. To this extent it might be argued that the monster is a personification of Burke's natural sublime. Presumably, Sir Walter Scott, in the most perspicacious early review of *Frankenstein*, reacts to something similar about the monster when he notes "the mysterious sublimity annexed to his first appearance."[8]

The sense that the mountains, especially Mont Blanc, were somehow alive or the embodiment of a powerful spirit is one that Mary Shelley seems to have shared with, and perhaps derived from, her husband. Between July 21st and July 27th, 1816, the Shelleys (in the company of a maid and Claire) visited the area around the village of Chamonix which figures so prominently in *Frankenstein*. Mary's *Journal*, silent for the preceding months, contains a detailed description of the *Mer de Glace* and Mont Blanc, a description that dovetails perfectly with that in the Frankenstein episode she wrote two days after returning to the Villa Chapuis. But this episode also parallels Percy Shelley's reaction to the experience as recorded in a letter to Thomas Love Peacock and in the poem written shortly thereafter entitled "Mont Blanc." In the portion of a letter to Peacock written July 25, 1816, Shelley concluded "that Mont Blanc was a living being & that the frozen blood forever circulated slowly thro' his stony veins."[9] The treatments of Mont Blanc and the surrounding region in Shelley's poem and in *Frankenstein* convey the same sense of animism. The documentary evidence might seem to support an argument that Shelley influenced Mary. However, this sense of presence in nature and the corresponding philosophical perplexities regarding the perceiver's role in what may after all be an illusion, a mere pathetic fallacy, is Wordsworthian as well as Shelleyan, and I prefer to think that here Mary and Sheley were of one mind.

After the deaths of William and Justine, Frankenstein (in the company of Elizabeth and his father in the 1818 version, alone in the 1831 version) retreats to the mountains, following precisely the Shelleys' itinerary. As the 1831 version has it, he hopes "in the magnificence, the eternity of such scenes, to forget myself and my ephemeral, because human, sorrows." The eternal, it is implied, is also the inhuman. One sentence, original with the 1831 edition, characterizes the landscape presence in terms similar to those used in "Mont Blanc": "The immense mountains and precipices that overhung me on every side—the sound of the river raging among the rocks, and the dashing of the waterfalls around, spoke of a power mighty as Omnipotence—and I ceased to fear, or to bend before any being less almighty than that which had created and ruled the elements, here displayed in their most terrific guise" (p. 94). And the second of the two sentences following (present in both editions), describing how the scene "was augmented and rendered sublime by the mighty Alps, whose white and shining pyramids and domes towered above all, as belonging to another earth, the habitations of another race of beings" (pp. 94-95), overlaps directly with this portion of "Mont Blanc" where

> many a precipice,
> Frost and the Sun in scorn of mortal power
> Have piled: dome, pyramid, and pinnacle,

71

A city of death, distinct with many a tower
And wall impregnable of beaming ice.[10]

Some of the words from *Frankenstein* here coincide with Shelley's and, indeed, the idealized Dome is a key symbol in Shelley's poetry,[11] but there is nothing to indicate that the vision expressed is alien to Mary's treatment of sublime landscape throughout the book. The manuscript version of this passage exhibits no sign of Shelley's amending hand. Perhaps Shelley appropriated Mary's words.

In the next chapter (two days later in the 1818 version, one day later in the 1831 version), Frankenstein continues alone in Mary's and Shelley's footsteps: "The abrupt sides of vast mountains were before me, the icy wall of the glacier overhung me; a few shattered pines were scattered around." The glacier is the *Mer de Glace*. Mary's *Journal* entry for July 24th includes a reference to the "tops of scattered pines" and in "Mont Blanc" Shelley includes the observation (with regard to the frozen waters of the upper Arve beneath the glacier) that "vast pines are strewing/ Its destined path, or in the mangled soil/ Branchless and shattered stand."[12] The force that can leave trees "broken and strewed on the ground" (p. 97) is subtly personalized as a kind of monster. The cracking ice, which "reverberated along the mountains" "was ever and anon rent and torn, as if it had been but a plaything in their hands." The hands presumably belong to the mountains, "the assemblance of grand shapes," "these mighty friends" (p. 96).

But this anthropomorphism is surely just in Frankenstein's mind? The issue is raised in "Mont Blanc":

> Dizzy Ravine! .... And, When I gaze on thee,
> I seem as in a trance sublime and strange
> To muse on my own separate fantasy,
> My own, my human mind, which passively
> Now renders and receives fast influencings,
> Holding an unremitting interchange
> With the clear universe of things around—[13]

When Frankenstein recalls the original effect that "the tremendous and ever-moving glacier had produced upon my mind" (p. 97), something of the same epistemological ambiguity intrudes. Certainly it is the glacier which is physically moving but Frankenstein is talking primarily about an emotional effect on his own mind: it is the glacier which is moving him. The syntactical ambiguity of the phrase "ever-moving glacier"—it is this same glacier which causes pines to be broken and a general scene of chaos—might be regarded as a neat synecdoche for the book's philosophical indecision. Like the monster, the animated scenery exists both objectively and within Frankenstein's mind.

Observing that the amnesiac effect "of the awful and majestic in nature" (p. 93) on life's cares works best in solitude, Frankenstein begins the ascent of Montanvert, a peak to the northeast of Mont Blanc and separated from it by the *Mer de Glace*. After surveying the scene from the top of Montanvert, Frankenstein descends to the glacier where he is impressed by the "awful majesty" of Mont Blanc towering above the accompanying peaks. These peaks, locked in ice at their base, "shone in the sunlight over the clouds," clouds above which they appear to float. This paradoxical fusion of mobility and immobility is carried over into Frankenstein's address to what literally appear to be the disembodied spirits of the dead but what syntactically appear to be the "peaks" above the "clouds": "Wandering spirits, if indeed ye wander, and do not rest in your narrow beds, allow me this faint happiness, or take me, as your companion, away from the joys of life." This address to the mountain spirits—a culminating point in the ambiguous process of personification—elicits an immediate reply (that in the manuscript follows without a paragraph break): "As I said this, I suddenly beheld the figure of a man, at some distance, advancing towards me with superhuman speed." Its size exceeds that of a man just as Mont Blanc exceeds in size the other mountains. It is, of course, the monster but the monster now identified by association as the personification of a wandering mountain spirit. By means of a syntactic symbolism, the monster is presented as the product of Frankenstein's sublime reaction—his heart "swelled with something like joy"—to a "wonderful and stupendous scene" (p. 98). No wonder the monster recalls his being a "creature whose thoughts were once filled with sublime and transcendent visions of the beauty and majesty of goodness" (p. 221).

If the Alps and their Arctic analogue appear to be the monster's natural habitat that is surely because his being is bound up with the awe and terror provoked by such environments. Before the episode in which the monster is explicitly identified with Alpine sublimity, Frankenstein has an earlier glimpse of his creation against the same backdrop. By the flickering illumination of a mountain storm, the monster appears phantasmagorically swinging, like Tarzan, from peak to peak. In horror, Frankenstein asks: "Who could arrest a creature capable of scaling the overhanging sides of Mont Selêve?" (p. 77). The combination of static tableau and swift movement in Frankenstein's awareness of the monster's bounding movement is almost transferred to the massive immobility of a mountain by means of an associative pun, whether conscious or not, in the description of Mont Selêve as "a hill that *bounds* Plainpalais on the south" (p. 76; my italics). The difficulty of capturing the monster is compounded if a sense of at-homeness with untractable natural phenomena becomes actual identification: "one might as well try to overtake

73

the winds, or confine a mountain stream with a straw" (pp. 78-79). The winds, with which the monster is here associated, are elsewhere specified as being cold and blowing from the north.

Before first catching sight of the monster, Robert Walton feels "a cold northern breeze" (p. 15) play bracingly upon his cheeks. Frankenstein estimates that the wind which drove his skiff from the Orkneys towards Ireland was "northeast" (p. 171) but one of the Irish fishermen who found Clerval's corpse testifies that the observation of "a strong northerly blast rising" (p. 174) caused him and his fellows to head for the harbour. Assuming Frankenstein to be the murderer, the fishermen argue that the boat seen leaving the shore in the vicinity of the crime was Frankenstein's and that "the strong north wind that had arisen" (pp. 175-76) forced his return to more or less the place of departure. Symbolically, of course, the evidence is damning. It is absurdly coincidental that Frankenstein should have landed in the exact area where the monster killed Clerval unless external circumstances relate directly to the state of Frankenstein's consciousness. But, once again, it is not really a matter of choice. The landscape is both real and psychic. From the psychic point of view, the monster and his sublime environmental matrix are within Frankenstein, constitutive of his own reality. Given the overlap of sensational stimulus between the mountains and the monster, it is appropriate that Frankenstein should say of his sensations, "they weighed on me with a mountain's weight, and their excess destroyed my agony beneath them" (p. 149).

As James Rieger has demonstrated, the cold northerly winds take their place in a context of environmental symbolism which exactly mirrors Frankenstein's changing fortunes.[14] Movement north signals the ascendancy of cold intellect, movement south the progress of emotional warmth. Frankenstein and Elizabeth plan to spend their honeymoon in the south at Como but, with the Alps in the way, they have to sail in a northerly direction to Evian where Elizabeth is throttled by the monster. Previously, Frankenstein journeyed north to the Orkneys where he proposed to create a female counterpart for his monster. But the Orkneys and the Arctic are not the only northern analogues of the Alps. On the way to the Orkneys, Frankenstein and Clerval stop at the village of Mattock situated in an area that resembled "the scenery of Switzerland" and passing northward through Cumberland and Westmoreland, Frankenstein fancies himself "among the Swiss mountains" (p. 161). But, like other oppositions in *Frankenstein*, that of compass direction, the apparently contradictory import of movement south and north, undergoes subversion. In respect to the Arctic, the Alps lie well in the south and the funeral pyre that the monster projects for himself might be viewed as providing a conjunction of southern heat and northern cold. After all, the essential confusion in *Frankenstein* is one of location.

Where precisely should the sublime experience be located? I have noted that the monster speaks of himself as a "creature whose thoughts were once filled with sublime and transcendent visions of the beauty and majesty of goodness" (p. 221). Qualities associated with an externalized landscape seem here to be internalized. The sublime must be regarded as a clear-cut instance of that metaphoric process whereby man creates an intelligible image of the universe. The sublime depends upon man's apprehending consciousness. In an exemplary work, *The Romantic Sublime: Studies in the Structure and Psychology of Transcendence*, Thomas Weiskel posits a relationship between the sublime and sublimation.[15] My analysis of the sublime setting in *Frankenstein* as something both real and within the protagonist's head points to the same semantic crossover.

Perhaps the phrase "all at sea" best indicates the occasions where Frankenstein's consciousness and his environment are most obviously continuous. I have referred to movement north and south. Very often that movement is accomplished by sea. The image of a boat on water constantly recurs. We are to infer, as Martin Tropp realizes, the traditional symbolic relationship between the fragile shell of consciousness and the depths of the mind.[16] Frankenstein's moments of calm sailing on Lac Léman following his marriage to Elizabeth are illusory or short-lived at best. More indicative of the true state of things is Frankenstein's terrifying experience aboard the wind-driven skiff which, of its own volition, takes him (and presumably his monster) from the Orkneys to a conspicuously unidentified town in Ireland: "The wind was high, and the waves continually threatened the safety of my little skiff" (p. 171). As the Alps are to the Arctic, so Lac Léman is to the turbulent ocean. The image of Frankenstein submitting to the elements of sea and wind signifies the relinquishment of control to his unconscious, the monster from the depths.

Frankenstein recalls that, during the final Arctic pursuit, "I often heard the thunder of the ground sea, which threatened my destruction" (p. 207). No wonder Frankenstein repeatedly appears as a wrecked ship. He impresses Walton as "a noble creature in his better days, being now in wreck so attractive and amiable" (p. 27). "Strange and harrowing must be his story; frightful the storm which embraced the gallant vessel on its course, and wrecked it—thus!" (p. 31). Frankenstein refers to "the storm ... hanging in the stars" (p. 42) and about to envelop him, and how he is beset by a "hurricane" of "feelings which bore me onwards" (p. 54). By his own account, Frankenstein "grew alarmed at the wreck I perceived that I had become" (p. 56). Not

75

much else in the landscape had changed but "*I* was a wreck" (p. 94), Frankenstein affirms, "a miserable spectacle of wrecked humanity" (p. 100).

No less than the moon and the mountains, the image of a broiling ocean is evocative of a subliminal sublime. Thomas Burnet's three "greatest Objects of Nature" are united in ways other than their common effect. The mountain glacier giving onto "the sea of ice," the *Mer de Glace,* is of uneven surface, "rising like the waves of a troubled sea, descending low, and interspersed by rifts that sink deep" (p. 98). And, of course, it is surely relevant if unobserved in *Frankenstein,* that the tidal influence of the moon contributes to the creation of troubled seas. In fact, in detailing the spheres of influence that bind together the moon, the monster, the mountains, Frankenstein and the sea, I have reversed what might be regarded as the most natural order. It makes some sense to see a circulating sublime power passing from the sea through Frankenstein, through the mountains, through the monster, through the moon and from the moon back to the sea again. At one moment it is within Frankenstein or the monster, at the next it is a function of the external environment.

This sublime power is uniquely creative and, if we are indeed to intuit an analogy between Mary Shelley's creation of the book *Frankenstein* and Frankenstein's creation of the monster, should we not look for a similar source of creativity in both cases? I have said that the monster is as much or perhaps more a creation of that sublime setting as he is of the laboratory. Is the book's creation as much a consequence of time spent appreciating an impressive environment as of time spent in an enclosed study? In her 1831 Introduction, Mary Shelley recalls her childhood visits to Scotland when she stayed with the Baxters:

> my habitual residence was on the blank and dreary northern shore of the Tay, near Dundee. Blank and dreary on restrospection I call them; they were not so to me then. They were the eyry of freedom . . . where unheeded I could commune with the creatures of my fancy. I wrote then, but in a commonplace style. It was beneath the trees of the grounds belonging to our house, or on the bleak sides of the woodless mountains near, that my true compositions, the airy flights of my imagination were born and fostered . . . I could people the hours with creations far more interesting to me at that age, than my own sensations. (p. 6)

Except, of course, that her "creations" and her "sensations" were not so separate after all.

In the body of *Frankenstein,* Mary's mountain-fostered creations are shared by Elizabeth in a context that pairs them with Frankenstein's ambitions:

She busied herself with following the aerial creations of the poets; and in the majestic and wondrous scenes which surrounded our Swiss home—the sublime shapes of the mountains; the changes of the seasons, tempest and calm; the silence of winter, and the life and turbulence of our Alpine summers,—she found ample scope for admiration and delight. While my companion contemplated with a serious and satisfied spirit the magnificent appearances of things, I delighted in investigating their causes. The world was to me a secret which I desired to define. Curiosity, earnest research to learn the hidden laws of nature, gladness akin to rapture, as they were unfolded to me, are among the earliest sensations I can remember. (p. 36)

Once again, "creations" and "sensations" seek a euphoneous conjunction. This passage constitutes Mary's elaboration of two sentences that Shelley wrote which appeared in the 1818 edition: "I delighted in investigating the facts relative to the actual world; she busied herself in following the aërial creations of the poets. The world was to me a secret, which I desired to discover; to her it was a vacancy, which she sought to people with imaginations of her own."[17] The effect of Mary's recasting is to soften the opposition, to emphasize the relevance of "the actual world" to both Mary's "creations" and Frankenstein's "sensations." The "creations" of the poet combine with the "sensations" of the scientist. It should be observed here that the issue raised is broadly philosophical and specifically germane to the overall meaning of *Frankenstein*.

(ii) *Magnetism*

In the interests of economy and dramatic directness, the encompassing story of Walton's polar exploration is usually omitted in the *Frankenstein* films. The famous Boris Karloff version opens with Frankenstein collecting his grisly anatomical bits and pieces. If the basic story can be related without the Walton subplot, it is not unreasonable to wonder about the aesthetic relevance of that aspect of Mary's book. Indeed, that most sensitive and exhaustive of Mary Shelley's critics, Jean de Palacio, cites with approval the view that Walton's letters are extraneous to Frankenstein's narrative.[18] I believe that Palacio is wrong: the Walton envelope is essential to the book's overall unity and design.

As has been observed, to a degree Walton is a double or reflection of Frankenstein. Like Frankenstein, he is in the grip of a scientific ambition which competes with the enjoyment of human relationships. Confronted with the consequences of Frankenstein's ambition, Walton is apparently persuaded to reverse his priorities. Walton is, then, certainly not extraneous to Mary Shelley's moral argument. Furthermore, it might be argued that as the person for whom Frankenstein's career provides an object lesson, Walton is a stand-in for the reader, a connecting link whereby the real world might appear to complete the series of concentric circles formed by the literary world of the text.

But more to the point is the fact that Walton's specific goal allows Mary Shelley to expand metaphorically on the import of Frankenstein's creation. Walton's quest for the North Pole and Frankenstein's interest in animating dead flesh are symbolically equivalent. The connecting link here is electromagnetism. When Mary wrote *Frankenstein* the relationship between magnetism and electricity was appreciated but imperfectly understood. For example, mesmerism was called animal magnetism because it was thought to depend on universal fields of influence, electrical fluids of a vaguely biochemical nature. However, from the point of view of electro-magnetic theory, the essential point is that all electrical currents create magnetic fiields. At the North Pole, Walton hopes to "discover the wondrous power which attracts the needle," to ascertain "the secret of the magnet" (p. 16), while Frankenstein relies on electricity to jolt his creation into life. The "secret of the magnet" is the secret of life itself. Any phallic connotations in Walton's phrase, "the wondrous power which attracts the needle," are entirely appropriate. The secret of life might well be imagined in sexual terms. The secret of life is also the secret of reality. Thus when Frankenstein reveals that "The world was to me a secret which I desired to divine" (p. 36) he is speaking about the same secret. And given the galvanizing role of "animal magnetism" in this story about a man who discovers the secret of life, the polar destination is inevitable.

Now is the time to emphasize what is perhaps the most potent aspect of the analogy I am pursuing between the creation of the book and the creation of the monster. If electricity animates the monster, it was talk of electricity that sparked Mary's creation. In her Introduction, she recalls listening to Byron and Shelley discuss "the principle of life" and "the experiments of Dr. Erasmus Darwin" (p. 8). Reportedly, Darwin "preserved a piece of vermicelli in a glass case, till by some extraordinary means it began to move with voluntary motion." Mary goes on to speculate that "Perhaps a corpse would be reanimated; galvanism had given token of such things: perhaps the component parts of a creature might be manufactured, brought together, and endued with vital warmth" (p. 9). In experimenting with the effects of electricity on the nervous systems of animals and human beings, Darwin was specifically indebted to Luigi Galvani (1737-1798) who gave his name to the galvanic electricity of which Mary speaks. It was Galvani's wife who, in 1786, drew his attention to the convulsive movements of a dead skinned frog.

Accidentally, the exposed nerves in one of the frog's legs touched a scalpel which had in turn become charged by contact with an electrical apparatus.

How much knowledge did Mary have of such matters? She lived at a time when scientific interest in the phenomena of electricity was producing new theories and new applications at an accelerating rate. Between the invention of the Leyden bottle (1745-46) and Faraday's electromagnetic rotation theory (1831, the year in which the revised *Frankenstein* appeared) that provided the basis of the dynamo together with the motor and electrical industry, Franklin proved that lightning is electricity by experimenting with kites (1760), Galvani observed "animal electricity" (1786), Count Alessandro Volta (1745-1827) created the "Voltaic Pile," the first battery (1800), and Sir Humphrey Davy (1778-1829) gave his acclaimed lecture "On the Chemical Effects of Electricity" (1806). As noted in Chapter 2, Mary records reading what appears to be Davy's *Elements of Chemical Philosophy* towards the end of October, 1816, that is, while she was writing what probably became Chapter 2 of *Frankenstein*.[19]

Shelley, of course, was fascinated by the subject of electricity since his time at Eton when he became interested in the galvanic battery and no doubt Mary would have acquired a certain amount of knowledge from him. When, in 1810, Jefferson Hogg stumbled into Shelley's rooms in University College, he found a scene remarkably suggestive of Frankenstein's laboratory as cinematically imagined, even allowing for some exaggeration in his eventual description. From the confusion of books and instruments it appears

> as if the young chemist, in order to analyse the mystery of creation had endeavoured first to re-construct the primeval chaos. The tables and especially the carpet, were already stained with large spots of various hues, which frequently proclaimed the agency of fire. An electrical machine, an air pump, the galvanic trough, a solar microscope, and large glass jars and receivers were conspicuous amidst the mass of matter.

After a while liquid being treated in a retort "boiled over, adding fresh stains to the table, and rising in fumes with a most disagreeable odour."[20] On another occasion, according to Hogg's recollection of their conversation, Shelley exclaimed: "What a mighty instrument would electricity be in the hands of him who knows how to wield it, in what manner to direct its omnipotent energies; . . . how many of the secrets of nature would such a stupendous force unlock!"[21] There can be no question that Shelley would have had much to contribute to the philosophical conversation that Mary recalls in her Introduction.

But was Shelley in conversation with Byron as Mary claims? James Rieger believes not. He follows the tentative suggestion of W. M. Rossetti in arguing that it was Polidori and not Byron who discussed "the principle of life" (p. 8) with Shelley.[22] Since Mary's *Journal* is blank for the period from May 14, 1815, to July 20, 1816, Polidori's diary provides the best documentary record of the time when *Frankenstein* was conceived and his entry for June 15, 1816, notes that in the evening "Shelley and I had a conversation about principles, —whether man was to be thought merely an instrument."[23] I see no reason to conclude as Rieger does that "This is almost certainly the conversation alluded to by Mary Shelley" in her Introduction.[24] That she refers to "the principle of life" as the subject of the conversation and that he speaks of "principles" counts for very little. The conversation that Polidori records involving the possibility that man is an instrument might well have been about fate and free will rather than the principles of galvanic electricity. Rieger wishes to suggest that the inspirational vision followed the discussion on the 15th of June and thus predated Byron's proposal of a ghost-story competition which Rieger believes occurred the following day. To make this case Rieger uses the dubious strategy of moving from provable inaccuracies in the Introduction—Mary's summary of a story from Jean Baptiste Benôit Eyries' *Fantasmagoriana* (1812)—to assumed ones.

There is no overpowering reason to doubt that the conversation Mary recalls took place between Shelley and Byron and that it transpired after the ghost-story competition was proposed. At the same time, even if Polidori was not present at that particular conversation, it is surely possible that he had at some point given either Byron or Shelley or both the benefit of his specialized knowledge on the subject of electricity. Not only was Polidori a first rate, newly-qualified physician but he had, in 1815, published a treatise on sleep-walking, a trance-like state which he and others attributed to the hypnotic effects of "animal magnetism." And during the last week of June, 1816, when Mary and Polidori (nursing a sprained ankle) were thrown into each other's company while Byron and Shelley toured Lac Léman (whether or not any indiscretions took place[25]), it is surely possible that the topic of electrical influences might have arisen again. It seems likely, then, that Mary acquired at least a rudimentary scientific knowledge from both Shelley and Polidori as well as from her reading of Davy.

The matter is important because at issue is the degree to which *Frankenstein* transformed the nature of the gothic romance. To what extent might it be described retrospectively as science fiction? Is it, as R. Glynn Grylls claims, "the first of the Scientific Romances?"[26] Presumably the assumption is that had Frankenstein retained his early enthusiasm for Cornelius Agrippa, Albertus Magnus and Paracelsus, and animated his creation by alchemical or supernatural means, the book would belong within traditional gothic confines. It is the assumption that Frankenstein employs contemporary science that invites the sense of a generic transfer into the realm of science fiction.

The Preface which Shelley wrote as the putative author of the original edition of *Frankenstein* opens with reference to this transfer:

> The event on which this fiction is founded, has been supposed, by Dr. Darwin, and some of the physiological writers of Germany, as not of impossible occurrence. I shall not be supposed as according the remotest degree of serious faith to such an imagination; yet, in assuming it as the basis of a work of fancy, I have not considered myself as merely weaving a series of supernatural terrors. The event on which the interest of the story depends is exempt from the disadvantages of a mere tale of spectres or enchantment.[27]

Possibly influenced by this Preface and certainly assuming Shelley to be the author of *Frankenstein*, Sir Walter Scott begins his review by describing the novel and its literary kin in a way that seems remarkably prescient of Wellsian science fiction. *Frankenstein* is included amongst those works where the marvellous is presented not for its own sake, as in the case of "Tom Thumb," but for its probable effect on human beings, as in the case of Gulliver's "Voyage to Brobdingnag": "we grant the extraordinary postulate which the author demands as the foundations of his narrative, only on condition of his deducing the consequences with logical precision."[28] Superficially, there can be no question that there is indeed a science-fictional feel about *Frankenstein* but I would hesitate before classifying it outright as science fiction and I would certainly not want to argue that *Frankenstein* is the first such work. As befits a scientific rather than a supernatural genre, the soul of science fiction did not suddenly descend as Brian Aldiss would have it; rather, contemporary science fiction is the result of successive stages of evolution. *Frankenstein* might be regarded as one evolutionary breakthrough.

The problem with regarding *Frankenstein* as straight science fiction is that, although the monster is apparently animated by scientific means, that science is treated by Mary Shelley in a metaphoric manner that owes more to the occult, superstitious "sciences", that Victor supposedly moves away from, than to any of the modern hard sciences that he apparently pursues. As will become clear, the scientific element in *Frankenstein*—the imagistic use of magnetism and electricity—suggests a well-nigh alchemical realm of transcendence. It serves the ends of sublimity. In fact, like most of the ostensibly exclusive oppositions in *Frankenstein*, that between alchemy and science is both real and illusory.

Frankenstein's enthusiasm for natural philosophy began when he picked up "a volume of the works of Cornelius Agrippa". In spite of his father's claim that such rubbish is a waste of time, Victor continues to study "the wild fancies" (p. 39) of Agrippa, Paracelsus and Albertus Magnus. As John A. Dussinger suggests, Frankenstein's subsequent career can be regarded as a rebellion against the rationalistic world represented by his father."[29] In support of this symbolic possibility, Dussinger resorts to the 1818 text which includes an episode excised in the 1831 version in which Victor's father demonstrates that lightning is electricity by repeating Franklin's experiment with a kite. Presumably the episode went because of a related annotation that Mary Shelley addresses to Frankenstein in the copy she gave to Mrs. Thomas: "you said your family was not scientific."[30] And so he did. In the 1831 version, after Frankensein's specification that "My father was not scientific" (p. 40), "a man of great research in natural philosophy" (p. 4) is briefly introduced to provide the information previously put in the mouth of Victor's father. It would appear that Frankenstein's rebellion against the narrow rationalism of his father is not necessarily a rebellion against science. Similarly, at university in Ingolstadt, Frankenstein reacts negatively to the closed mind of Professor Krempe who dismisses the alchemists' works as "nonsense" (p. 45) but positively to Professor Waldman who argues that the expansive spirit of the ancient alchemists is not incompatible with the methodology of modern science.

Radu Florsecu quotes with approval Rieger's conclusion that "it would be a mistake to call *Frankenstein* a pioneer work of science fiction. Its author knew something of Sir Humphrey Davy's chemistry, Erasmus Darwin's botany, and perhaps Galvani's physics, but little of this got into her book. Frankenstein's chemistry is switched-on magic, souped-up alchemy, the electrification of Agrippa and Paracelsus."[31] However, eleven years earlier Rieger seems to have concluded differently. His article, "Dr. Polidori and the Genesis of *Frankenstein*," includes the assertion that "*Frankenstein* may be vulgarly termed science fiction."[32] The truth is that generically *Frankenstein* occupies a place on the borders of science fiction and other forms of what I have elsewhere defined as apocalyptic literature.[33] It "transcends" the genre of science fiction. In my terms, apocalyptic writers create other worlds which, by virtue of a reading convention, exist (on a literal level) in a credible relationship with the "real" world as commonly understood. This credibility depends upon overtures to either reason or a religious kind of faith. It will be apparent that this formulation includes both serious science fiction and such works as the *Divine Comedy* and *Paradise Lost*. To conceive of the category "apocalyptic literature" is to appreciate immediately how the structure and concerns of science fiction parallel, slide into, or may be embraced by, structures of transcendence. *Frankenstein* is very much a case in point and hence Rieger's contradictory statements. *Frankenstein* cannot be accounted for as science fiction with any degree of comprehensibility because, as Florescu states, "Mary's monster is more the child of the alchemists and occultists than of the scientists."[34]

The alchemical promise of immortality which obsesses Frankenstein seems to have at least intrigued Mary Shelley. Two of her tales and a speculative essay deal variously with the theme of extended life. In "The Mortal Immortal" (1833), the topic is linked directly to alchemy. Winzy, an assistant of Cornelius Agrippa, is writing his account three centuries after having drunk and then spilled his master's magical beverage. Immortality turns out to be a curse and despairingly Winzy looks at himself for signs of mortality and decay.

Two related pieces treat the kindred theme of reanimation. An unfinished tale, entitled by Charles E. Robinson "Valerius: The Reanimated Roman,"[35] is silent about the process of revival but explicit about Valerius's depressive reaction to the declined condition of nineteenth-century Rome. In mood and theme this story of the last true Roman is clearly anticipative of Mary's *The Last Man* (1826). "Roger Dodsworth: The Reanimated Englishman" is Charles E. Robinson's title for a piece he recently discovered that Mary wrote in response to a contemporary hoax.[36] It was submitted for publication to the *New Monthly Magazine* in 1826 but not printed until 1863 when it appeared without a title in a volume of reminiscenses by an editor of the *New Monthly Magazine.* Supposedly Dodsworth "died" in 1654 in circumstances that kept him in a frost-locked state of suspended animation. This detail plus the concluding paragraphs, in which Mary speculates on the possibilities if we all remembered previous lives, make the Dodsworth piece the most science-fictional of her writings. The only alchemical change relevant here is that the Dodsworth essay is a particularly clear indication of the way in which certain hoaxical forms and incidents become transmuted into science fiction.[37]

Essentially Frankenstein was drawn to the alchemists because, in their ambitions, they transcended human limitations, they "sought immortality and power" (p. 46). Under their guidance, "I entered with the greatest diligence into the search of the philosopher's stone and the elixir of life; but the latter soon obtained my undivided attention." Symbolically, the transformation of lead into gold betokens the transmutation of the alchemist from a physical to a presumably eternal spiritual state. To a degree, then, Frankenstein is posing a false dichotomy. No less than the elixir of life, the philosopher's stone promises immortality. The effect is to blur the equation between immortality and transcendence. A corresponding confusion characterizes Frankenstein's subsequent pronouncement: "Wealth was an inferior object; but what glory would attend the discovery, if I could banish disease from the human frame and render man invulnerable to any but a violent death!" (p. 40). In the pursuit of the philosopher's stone, which is here seemingly rejected, wealth is equally an inferior object and the reward of eternal life renders man invulnerable to death per se. The creation of the monster is linked to something much grander—life after death, the resurrection of the body: "Life and death appeared to me ideal bounds, which I should first break through, and pour a torrent of light into our dark world...I thought that if I could bestow animation upon lifeless matter, I might in process of time...renew life where death had apparently devoted the body to corruption" (p. 54). Frankenstein seeks the power of God on the day of resurrection. No wonder that Chevalier's frontispiece for the 1831 edition (reproduced following this page), depicting a revitalized figure in a chapel-like laboratory,[38] appears to owe as much to the biblical raising of Lazarus as to the details of Mary Shelley's text.

It should, in fact, be emphasized that, from the start, Frankenstein's ambitions are of a paradoxical mix of the material and the spiritual: "It was the secrets of heaven and earth that I desired to learn; and whether it was the outward substance of things, or the inner spirit of nature and the mysterious soul of man that occupied me, still my inquiries were directed to the metaphysical, or, in its highest sense, the physical secrets of the world" (p. 37). Here is a particularly brazen instance of that solipsistic dissolution of distinction which might be considered a stylistic trademark of *Frankenstein*. If the essential distinction between a perceiving consciousness and an exterior reality is lost, what other distinctions can hold? And so we are encouraged to understand the physical and the metaphysical not as opposites but as synonyms.

It is the function of the sublime ingredients in *Frankenstein* to make this conjunction of the transcendent and the material, the secular and the sacred, metaphorically manifest. Mary's treatment of electricity and magnetism is among those sublime ingredients. Electricity is to the Alps as magnetism is to the Arctic wastes. The lure of magnetism that leads Walton to the ends of the earth, to "a country of eternal light" (p. 16), is symbolically akin to the electrical discharges which cause the Alps in a stormy summer to be illuminated by lightning. In one dramatic scene, the lightning and Mont Blanc are procreatively wedded.

Returning to Geneva in response to the news of William's death, Frankenstein "was obliged to cross the lake in a boat to arrive at Plainpalais. During this short voyage I saw the lightnings playing on the summit of Mont Blanc in the most beautiful figures" (p. 75). The ambiguity of "figures" is deliberate. Amidst this sublime tempest, "so beautiful yet terrific," making the lake from the land appear, like Milton's Hell, "a vast sheet of fire," one figure

Frontispiece to the 1831 Edition by W. Chevalier

soon detaches itself: "I perceived in the gloom a figure which stole from behind a clump of trees near me ... A flash of lightning illuminated the object and discovered its shape plainly to me; its gigantic stature, and the deformity of its aspect, more hideous than belongs to humanity, instantly informed me that it was the wretch, the filthy daemon to whom I had given life." Its appearance follows immediately on Frankenstein's almost exultant apostrophe to the storm: "William, dear angel! this is thy funeral, this thy dirge!" (p. 76). In the colloquial sense, it is the monster who is William's funeral and the effect of the syntax and the word "figures" is to equate the monster with the overall spectacle. This scene is a symbolic analogue to that in which Frankenstein infused "a spark of being into the lifeless thing that lay at my feet" (p. 57). Lightning electrifies the Alps and gives life to the sublime Alpine qualities that the monster might be said to personify. If (as I have suggested in my discussion of Mary's literary sources) the time-lapse impression of the monster's bounding movements from crag to crag echoes the action of the thunder in Byron's *Childe Harold*, an association between the monster and the elements is also to be inferred. Indeed, on a later occasion, the monster, after "running with the swiftness of lightning, plunged into the lake" (p. 196).

This scene is twice recreated making it an example, and perhaps the most important one, of that thrice-used technique of "metamorphic duplication." In the other two instances, however, a scene is recreated only once. The case of a Swiss landscape fusing with a German one is treated in Chapter 2. And the two occasions when the monster is presented hovering over the body of prone Frankenstein are discussed in Chapter 3. The basic purpose of this technique is to convey a sense of unity in a situation where separation is more apparent. In the case of the scene with which we are presently concerned what is mirrored or prefigured first of all is Frankenstein's next meeting with his creation, an episode that I emphasized in dealing with the function of the sublime setting.

In that episode Frankenstein is in the immediate vicinity of Mount Blanc, but otherwise events transpire as before. The same formulaic sequence applies: an elevation of spirits, a direct address to the spirit world, the immediate appearance of the monster. Here is the context of the first encounter:

This noble war in the sky elevated my spirits; I clasped my hands, and exclaimed aloud, "William, dear angel! this is thy funeral, this thy dirge!" As I said these words, I perceived in the gloom a figure ... (p. 76)

And here is the context of the second encounter:

My heart, which was before sorrowful, now swelled with something like joy; I exclaimed—"Wandering spirits, if indeed ye wander, and do not rest in your narrow beds, allow me this faint happiness, or take me, as your companion, away from the joys of life."

As I said this I suddenly beheld the figure of a man ... (p. 98)

Not only is the succession of events the same but so are several of the actual words and phrases. This parallelism provides the clearest evidence that Mary Shelley wished to convey the notion that Frankenstein, the Alpine setting and the monster may be considered as a continuum. The experience of sublimity created within Frankenstein by the setting calls the monster into being. And since electricity is the source of life, it is surely not accidental that, at the end of the chapter before that in which Frankenstein meets his monster for the second time, he watches "the pallid lightnings that played above Mont Blanc" (p. 95) before submitting to the oblivion of sleep. The monster as originally described is somewhat pallid and unhealthy looking.

The situation in which an address by Frankenstein to the spirit world is answered immediately by the appearance of the monster is duplicated a second time shortly after the murder of Elizabeth and the death of his father. Standing by the graves (or what are referred to in the indented quotation above as the "narrow beds") of William, Elizabeth and his father, Franken-stein is conscious of "The spirits of the departed ..." "I knelt on the grass, and kissed the earth, and with quivering lips exclaimed [this word is used in the two previous similar episodes], 'By the sacred earth on which I kneel, by the shades that wander near me ... I swear ... to pursue the daemon, who caused this misery until he or I shall perish in mortal conflict." The tangible earth and the intangible spirit world are here united. Becoming increasingly enraged (a *heightening* of depressed spirits if not exactly an elevation as in the two previous episodes, the imminent appearance of the monster is simi-larly associated with a change of mental state), Frankenstein continues: "And I call on you, spirits of the dead, and on you, wandering ministers of ven-geance, to aid and conduct me in my work." Immediately, "I was answered through the stillness of night by a loud and fiendish laugh" which "the moun-tains re-echoed ..." Momentarily, "I felt as if all hell surrounded me" but the voice which whispers "close to my ear" (p. 202) he recognizes as that of his monster.

This scene juxtaposes four apparent realities—Frankenstein's psyche, the natural world, the spirit world and the monster—in a way that casts doubt upon their existence as separable entities. It should further be observed that an electrical storm is present here but completely internalized, created by the discharging neurons within Frankenstein's skull: "the furies possessed me as

I concluded, and rage choked my utterance." Some evidence of this internal tempest is provided by the reference to the spirits (one is tempted to visualize them as lightning flashes) which "seemed to flit around, and to cast a shadow which was felt but not seen, around the head of the mourner" (p. 202).

Frankenstein first became aware of the power of electricity—its destructive rather than creative aspect—when he was "about fifteen years old." During a violent thunderstorm, "I beheld a stream of fire issue from an old and beautiful oak ... and so soon as the dazzling light vanished, the oak had disappeared, and nothing remained but a blasted stump." The tree itself "was not splintered by the shock, but entirely reduced to thin ribbons of wood. I never beheld anything so utterly destroyed" (p. 41). Although this episode is in both the 1818 and the 1831 versions, the successive paragraphs differ. At the end of the new succession of paragraphs which Mary wrote for the 1831 edition, an equation is insinuated between the blasted tree and Frankenstein's fate. Although diverted from his alchemical obsessions for a while, "Destiny was too potent, and her immutable laws had decreed my utter and terrible destruction" (p. 42). Like the tree, Frankenstein is to be "utterly destroyed." As Frankenstein later observes, "I am a blasted tree; the bolt has entered my soul" (p. 160); the same comparison applies when Frankenstein speaks of his creation daring "again to blast me" (p. 183) and of himself as "one blasted and miserable" (p. 190). Specifically, he has been "blasted" (p. 218) in his hopes of scientific distinction. The blasted tree is to Frankenstein as the Alps are to the monster. In both cases, a being and an aspect of the external environment are confused.

The destructive aspect of electricity and lightning manifests itself as fire and thereby the monster also learns about its dangerous nature. Attracted by the heat of an abandoned fire, the monster thrusts his hand into the live embers. The discovery of pain causes the monster to reflect, with puzzlement, "that the same cause should produce such opposite effects!" The Promethean flame is an ambiguous gift. Soon he realizes that "the fire gave light as well as heat" (p. 105) and pain. The words in which the monster projects his final immolation affirms that such diverse aspects may indeed be united: "Soon these burning miseries will be extinct. I shall ascend my funeral pile triumphantly, and exult in the agony of the torturing flames. The light of that conflagration will fade away; my ashes will be swept into the sea by the winds" (p. 223).[39] And a region of deathly cold will have known, if only fleetingly, the warmth of life. The central apocalyptic images of fire and ice will have been reconciled. However, that apocalypse is not dramatized. The only use the monster actually makes of fire is purely destructive. Out of feelings of rejection he sets alight the De Lacey cottage at the symbolic moment that the moon's light sinks below the western horizon: "The wind fanned the fire, and the cottage was quickly enveloped by the flames, which clung to it, and licked it with their forked and destroying tongues" (p. 139). A convincing facsimile of an Edenic world is obliterated.

But it is, in fact, as an apocalyptic source of light and revelation that electricity and magnetism are primarily valued. Frankenstein's discovery of the secret of life is presented as a religious relevation: "from the midst of darkness a sudden light broke upon me—a light so brilliant and wondrous, yet so simple, that ... I became dizzy with the immensity of the prospect which it illustrated ..." (p. 52). Apparently the secret of life is of a spiritual nature and its discovery involves the experience of transcendence: "Life and death appeared to me as ideal bounds, which I should first break through, and pour a torrent of light into our dark world" (p. 54). Electricity will serve to animate dead matter not because of any scientific rationale but because its nature is spiritual. The idea was not uncommon and indeed Volney's *Ruins of Empire*, the book Felix uses to teach Safie English, contains an allusion to that mystical doctrine: "the more I consider what the ancients understood by ether or spirit, and what the Indians call *akache*, the stronger do I find the analogy between it and the electrical fluid."[40]

It is as an embodiment of the spiritual power of electricity that Frankenstein repeatedly calls his creation a "daemon" not, as several modern texts would have it, a "demon."[41] This corruption radically falsifies Mary's intention. The modern reader, seeing the word "demon" will understand it to mean some kind of fiend or evil being. As originally spelt and as Mary Shelley uses it, the word "daemon" also means a spiritual power, irrespective of its moral nature. The point needs emphasizing that, in going beyond human bounds, the territory in which Frankenstein finds himself is at least metaphorically spiritual.

No less than Frankenstein, Walton is after the ultimate secrets of Heaven and Earth. And magnetism, no less than electricity, promises the secret of life, of animation. The pervasive use of such words as "animation" and "animated," to which I have already drawn attention, stresses the fact that life is movement. Because the earth revolves around its polarized axis, magnetism might be said to give movement—animation—to dead inert matter. The spiritual nature of Walton's ambitions is subtly emphasized. They cause his heart to glow "with an enthusiasm which elevates me to heaven." Walton's enthusiasm had been given a romantic colouring by his reading "those poets whose effusions entranced my soul, and lifted it to heaven. I also became a poet, and lived for one year in a Paradise of my own creation" (p. 17). Similarly, Frankenstein recalls, "I trod heaven in my thoughts" (p. 211). It should be noted that Walton's first letter is addressed from St. Petersburgh and his second from Archangel, place names which M. A. Goldberg realizes are "hardly fortuitous."[42] They point to the spiritual realm of Frankenstein's and Walton's ambitions, and perhaps, if Frankenstein's subsequent comparison between himself and "the archangel who aspired to omnipotence" (p. 211) is judged relevant, to a "noble war in the sky" (p. 76), a confrontation of the ultimate forces of good and evil.

The light of life is an unearthly one and its source somewhere very like that place in the sky, a place beyond the rim of the world. Thus, "the ever-moving glacier" filled Frankenstein "with a sublime ectasy that gave wings to the soul, and allowed it to soar from the obscure world to light and joy" (p. 97). Walton expects to find at the North Pole "a country of eternal light" (p. 16) where "the sun is forever visible" (p. 17). In the copy Mary gave to Mrs. Thomas she corrected her scientific mistake and substituted for the words "of eternal light" the explanatory statement, "ruled by different laws and in which numerous circumstances enforce a belief that the aspect of nature differs essentially from any such thing of which we have any experience."[43] However, in the 1831 edition the error is allowed to stand, presumably on the basis of its symbolic appropriateness. The "country of eternal light" is a sublime region where natures of essentially different aspect, like the monster's, rule. It is that region "rendered sublime by the mighty Alps, where white and shining pyramids and domes towered above all, as belonging to another earth, the habitations of another race of beings" (p. 94-95), and that region referred to by the monster as "another world" (p. 101) which the sun illumines as it sinks behind the snowy mountain precipices.

I have drawn attention to the importance of compass directions in *Frankenstein* as indicative of intellectual or emotional dominance, and of the way in which that distinction is subtly inverted. At the pole where the compass points in all directions this process reaches its apotheosis.[44] All intellectual bearings are lost, knowledge is shown to be contradictory and problematical. The epistemological relevance of this for *Frankenstein* as a whole forms the subject of the next and final chapter. But if the source of magnetism throws human understanding into question, the possibility of a trancendent knowledge is left open and magnetism itself affirms the power of love and emotion. All of *Frankenstein* may be comprehended in terms of the symbolism of magnetism or the ideas related to magnetism. Magnetism is that force of attraction which draws things together, including both human beings and the seemingly disparate parts of Mary Shelley's creation.

CHAPTER FIVE

"Stupendous Mechanism": Reality as Metaphor

Frankenstein, Walton and the monster are all after knowledge and knowledge is what *Frankenstein* is all about. If science fiction is perversely understood strictly in terms of the Latin root, *scientia*, as knowledge fiction, then *Frankenstein* is science fiction. It asks questions about the nature of knowledge, its extent, its value and its reliability. Such questions are, of course, philosophical but, while the philosophical character of *Frankenstein* has been occasionally recognized, it has not been treated at any length.

The usual procedure is to note that Mary read Locke's *Essay Concerning Human Understanding* and adhered to his sensationalistic psychology in describing the monster's initial moments of awareness. Beyond that particular episode it would appear that a knowledge of Locke has little to add to the understanding of *Frankenstein*. It has been assumed that Mary took Locke pretty much at his word and that, since there is no direct evidence of her having read Berkeley and Hume at the time, she wrote in ignorance of the solipsistic philosophy which grew from what may be regarded as the cracks and contradictions of Locke's system. However, as I have attempted to indicate, much of *Frankenstein* raises the suspicion of a solipsistic reality and that pervasive sense of ontological doubt ultimately owes its existence to some of the more unsettling implications of Locke's philosophy.

Locke is commonly regarded not as a solipsist but as the founder of British empirical philosophy. His philosophical position is dualist: the mind of man exists and so does an external reality. However, the fact is that Locke's system does provide a basis for the idealist position that all reality is within the mind, a position towards which the work of his successors, Bishop George Berkeley and Davd Hume, inexorably moves.[1] Locke's argument begins with the denial of innate ideas. The mind at birth is a *tabula rasa*. Everything it comes to *know*, as distinct from what it may come to *believe*, derives from experience and subsequent reflection on that data. But the external world is not experienced directly; it is filtered through the senses which are compared with little openings in a darkened closet. What the mind has to reflect on, then, is not reality itself but what Locke calls, after some hesitation, "ideas" of things outside. An unknown world of "substance" external to the mind of man is somehow causally related to the world of "ideas" within the mind of man.

It was left to Berkeley and Hume to explore the alternative possibility that, if the world of "ideas" is not the external world of reality but only corresponds loosely to, or represents that world, there is no logical necessity to suppose the causal existence of that world. Berkeley's *Principles of Human Knowledge* (1710) claims that nothing exists apart from perception: *esse est percepi*. But compelled by his religious calling, Bishop Berkeley does not wish to dismiss the realm of perception as an illusion. He argues, in a neo-Platonic vein, that the perceived world of "ideas" is real as long as it is constituted by a continual act of perception on the part of God. David Hume, in *An Enquiry Concerning Human Understanding* (1748) has no religious axe to grind. He carries the empirical sensationalism of Locke and Berkeley to its conclusion and dismisses all talk of any reality beyond experience as meaningless. There is no Lockean "substance," only an enclosed world of variously associated "ideas" which gives the illusion of external reality. What is taken for causality is only a matter of association, a mechanical process.

Frankenstein makes most sense if it is interpreted not just in relation to Locke but in relation to that entire body of philosophy to which Locke gives rise. In Earl Wasserman's words, "Locke's unsatisfactory theory of substance and qualities, Berkeley's God-based idealism, and Hume's skepticism had bequeathed to the early nineteenth century a universe whose location and constitution were disturbingly uncertain; and the Romantic was inevitably challenged to define reality and the mind's relation to it if he was to live in any meaningful way and to settle on the nature and values of experience."[2] *Frankenstein* is Mary Shelley's response to that challenge. The evidence that Mary read Locke before and while writing *Frankenstein* is both helpful and misleading. It is misleading if it leads to the assumption that only Locke's philosophy is relevant to the meaning of *Frankenstein*. Locke was not troubled by the uncertainties that Wasserman describes and to read *Frankenstein* in the light of Locke's substantial certainties is to radically misconstrue the book.

Although there is no documentary evidence proving that, while writing *Frankenstein*, Mary was aware of the various revisionist philosophical systems subsequent to Locke, the indirect evidence is overwhelming. Discounting for the moment the evidence of Mary's text itself, there is the fact of her close association with a man who was profoundly concerned with the varieties of philosophical thought. Shelley's final philosophical position appears to be complexly eclectic, owing as much to Platonic and occultist thought as to the philosophies of Locke, Berkeley, Hume and others. But, according to Wasserman, between 1812 and 1816 when he wrote "Mont Blanc," Shelley moved from a Lockean dualism of mind and matter to a monistic ontology of mind that he occasionally called his "intellectual philosophy."[3] His reading of Berkeley particularly and of Hume seems to have precipitated this development. In a letter to Hogg dated November 26, 1813, Shelley acknowledges that "Hume's reasonings with respect to the non-existence of external things ... appear to me to follow from the doctrines of Locke."[4] It would be extraordinary to suppose that Mary Shelley was unaware of this revolution in Shelley's thought culminating during the two years they were together before she wrote *Frankenstein*. Even if Mary did not read Berkeley and Hume during that period she must have familiarized herself with their views from her familiarity with Shelley. Clearly Trelawny had reason to observe of Mary's "fine intellect" that "her head might be put upon the shoulders of a Philosopher."[5]

However, I do not wish to argue that the philosophical content of *Frankenstein* corresponds to Shelley's "intellectual philosophy." *Frankenstein* embodies what might be termed a philosophical or ontological plasticity which may be construed as including Shelley's position and others in an overall context of critique. It is in this context that the various uncertainties, which are highlighted by the kind of critical analysis that I have employed in the previous chapters, have their function. While Shelley's response to the air of ontological uncertainty in the early nineteenth century was to jerry-build a solution, Mary's response was to embrace that uncertainty. The troubling uncertainty about the nature of the Other, the possibility that the beloved and the monster are somehow self-reflexive doppelgängers and that love is therefore some kind of homosexual or incestuous self-abuse, are the means by which the book's "ontological plasticity" is dramatized. Thus we have a situation in which the Other does have tangible existence and can be both known and loved at the same time as one in which the Other is only an aspect of the self and both knowledge and love are forms of solipsism; a situation in which a known external reality does have an independent existence and one in which it does not; and finally a situation which implies the existence of the degrees of dualism and solipsism in between.

It is no wonder that basically *Frankenstein* is about the problematical nature of knowledge. The wonder is that amongst *Frankenstein*'s many critics only one, L. J. Swingle, has recognized the fact.[6] The central symbol of this final unknowability is, of course, the nameless monster. What cannot be named cannot be grasped, cannot be understood. In the course of the book, Frankenstein's construction is called a number of things—a fiend, a creature, a man, a monster, a daemon, a spirit, as well as simply a thing—and in his doppelgänger role, as we have seen, he might appropriately be called Frankenstein. But all of these appellations are provisional, equally true or equally false. Swingle argues that, as a type of the Stranger, the monster (let us agree for the sake of a convenient convention to use this term) presents a challenge to the structure of common human concerns, an invitation to form "a new, enlarged mental world."[7]

But if from the dualist viewpoint the introduction of the monster serves to throw conventional reality into doubt, then it is reality itself which becomes alien, strange and unknown. This kinship between the monster and human reality is ultimately manifested at the solipsistic end of the book's ontological spectrum where the reader is compelled to the recognition that the monster, in a real sense, *is* the corporeal world of human reality. From this point of view, *Frankenstein* provides a variation of an honourable literary tradition described in Leonard Barkan's recent book, *Nature's Work of Art: The Human Body as Image of the World*.[8] If we cannot get outside of our own skins then the outside universe which we mistakenly believe to exist is actually a projection of ourselves. As Shelley put it in his "Speculation on Metaphysics," (1815?) "that mass of knowledge ..., including our own nature, constitutes what we call the universe."[9] Reality assumes a monstrous, metaphorical human form. "Monstrous" is a synonym for "huge" and, although we are not told directly that Frankenstein's monster extends to the limits of the perceived universe, he is definitely outsize. Frankenstein explains that, in pursuing the "magnitude" of his plan, the "minuteness of the parts" called for an element of magnification: "I resolved ... to make the being of a gigantic stature; that is to say, about eight feet in height, and proportionately large" (p. 54). But this image of the corporeal universe is also insubstantial, a daemon. Shelley was interested in daemons and, indeed, a rehandled portion of *Queen Mab* is entitled "The Daemon of the World." Frankenstein's monster appears to be Mary Shelley's version of that Daemon.

The recognition that the monster may be our anthropomorphic reality proceeds logically from the analysis of the preceding two chapters. We have observed the evidence linking the monster, on the one hand, to Frankenstein's psyche in a way that may be viewed as comprehending the other human relationships in the book and, on the other, to the sublime aspects of the "external" world of moon, sea and mountains. At the same time, the sublime aspects of the "external" world gain their sublimity in relation to human standards and, as a projection of Frankenstein's subconscious, the sea appears to be particularly representative of those elements—thus, the sublime may be a sublimative mechanism. We are led to suspect a seamless, vicious circle of associative "ideas" within Frankenstein's head. Whether Frankenstein be construed as man particularized or Man generalized, the macrocosm appears to be contained within the human microcosm.

There are numerous details in *Frankenstein* that may be related to the idea that an anthropomorphic reality exists within the mind. It is implicit in the metaphoric use of the word "world" to describe a writer's *oeuvre*. At one point Frankenstein quotes from the "world" of Wordsworth's "Tintern Abby" in order to suggest the quality of Clerval's sensibility. But Clerval is now dead and, consequently, Frankenstein asks, "Has this mind, so replete with ideas, imaginations fanciful and magnificent, which formed a world, whose existence depended on the life of its creator;—has this mind perished?" (pp. 156-57). At other points the human microcosm provides a way of describing the macrocosm. Frankenstein asserts that "The most learned philosophers ... had partially unveiled the face of Nature, but her immortal lineaments were still a wonder and a mystery. He might dissect, anatomize, and give names; but, not to speak of a final cause, causes in their secondary and tertiary grades were utterly unknown to him" (p. 40). A similar corporeal analogy is hinted at in Professor Waldman's assertion that modern philosophers "have discovered how the blood circulates, and the nature of the air we breathe" (p. 48). Blood is to the body as air is to the world?

Frankenstein's creation (although essentially a matter of organization) is, then, directly comparable to God's Creation. It may even be God's Creation as heretically conceived.[10] There is a passage in Thoreau's *Walden* that reads as if it were directly inspired by this intuition of the meaning of *Frankenstein*. Standing by the railway cutting observing the action of the spring thaw, Thoreau senses himself to be in "the laboratory of the Artist who made the world and me."[11] The emphasis on the embryonic development of a fragmented but clearly organic anatomy (conveyed in a philologically-based punning style which serves to equate the fecundity of nature and language) suggests that the laboratory might well be Frankenstein's if viewed positively. What the entire description amounts to is a microcosmic version of Genesis —Creation out of Chaos.

By the phrase "Frankenstein's creation" should be understood not only the creation of the monster and the creation of a "known" universe but also the creation of a book. Through Frankenstein, Mary Shelley is able to demonstrate that the two mythic roles of Prometheus are actually identical. If the mould of man determines, to a lesser or greater degree, the mould of knowledge, it is singularly appropriate that the bringer of fire, the source of human knowledge, is also the shaper of man. But knowledge of a reality that exists within the human mind is indistinguishable from fiction. In a sense, then, the universe that Frankenstein creates is a fictional universe; it is like the universe that Mary Shelley creates. This correspondence may be intuited if we further understand the phrase "Frankenstein's creation" as referring either to Mary's creation of her character or, since Frankenstein (as spoken rather than as written) denotes ambiguously both the name of a scientist and the title of a book, her creation of a fictional world or universe.

My point is, simply, that the construction of the fictional world *Franken-stein*, the construction of the monster, and the construction of the human world are offered as analogues of one another. The extent to which the three areas of analogy are merely rough parallels and the extent to which they represent a fundamental identity is left open. But the possibility is strong that the monstrous make-up of human reality is to be attributed to a mechanistic psychology such as that on which the systems of Locke, Berkeley and Hume are founded. *Frankenstein*, generally, reflects a mechanistic view of the universe, that is, of a universe comprehended in materialist human terms. Given that the mechanical is, by definition, non-spiritual, the following account in Mary's Introduction of her inspirational vision is rather paradoxical: "I saw the hideous phantasm of a man stretched out, and then, on the working of some powerful engine, show signs of life and stir with an uneasy, half vital motion. Frightful must it be; for supremely frightful would be the effect of any human endeavour to mock the stupendous mechanism of the Creator of the world" (p. 9). The syntactic effect here is to equate Frankenstein's "hideous phantasm" with the "stupendous mechanism" of God's universe, to imply, in fact, that the monster corresponds to human reality. This fusion or, perhaps, confusion is enhanced by the effect of the actual words used. A "phantasm" is something insubstantial, perhaps something spiritual. The aura of spirituality, excluded by the concept of God's "stupendous mechanism," is associated with Frankenstein's creation. One is left with a sense of inversion that serves to relate the inverted objects. At the same time, a sub-textual logic would associate the stirring produced by "the working of some powerful engine" with the movement of a "stupendous mechanism" and that "stupendous mechanism" with Frankenstein's monster.

If Mary's reference four paragraphs earlier to "the machinery of a story" (p. 7) is then recalled, the reader is provided with an imagistic shorthand which serves to equate Mary's book, the monster and human reality. But it is within the body of *Frankenstein* that these mechanical phenomena become related to what Frankenstein calls "the mechanism of my being" (p. 48). When Frankenstein speaks of the deaths for which he feels his "machinations" (pp. 176, 186) responsible, is he not speaking of the plot which makes up the machinery of Mary Shelley's story? But any mechanical set-up is finally enclosed and deterministic. Thus Frankenstein comes to sense that "I pursued my path towards the destruction of the daemon more as a task enjoined by heaven, *as the mechanical impulse of some power of which I was unconscious,* than as the ardent desire of my soul" (p. 204; Shelley's addition italicized). The confusions here reflect Frankenstein's limited understanding of the psychological mechanisms whereby something for which one does not wish to acknowledge responsibility is externalized. In pursuing the daemon, he is following and not flouting the desire of his soul.

At bottom, then, what is implied by this mechanical imagery is a mechanistic conception of the human mind and not a literal machine. The point should be emphasized because of the anachronistic tendency to relate the monster to the robots of science fiction and make him a symbol of an anthropomorphic technology gone berserk. In fact the idea has become something of a cliché in *Frankenstein* criticism and is variously expounded by Small, Aldiss and Tropp.[12] In the last quarter of the twentieth century, we have good reason to fear the destructive potential of technology. Living in the first quarter of the nineteenth century, Mary Shelley could not have been troubled by such fears and there is no way a case can be substantiated from the text for seeing the monster as "the first . . . symbol of modern technology."[13] This reading is a matter of extrinsic significance generated by the temporal context of the twentieth century.[14] And it is very largely a consequence of the desire to label *Frankenstein* as science fiction. But as I have demonstrated, alchemy rather than science or technology is at the imagistic heart of *Frankenstein.*

However, the assertion that the monster be understood as technology on the rampage is an acknowledgement of the monster's metaphoric import. As Tropp observes, "*Frankenstein* is in fact built like a maze that leads further and further into itself while extending to the limits of the known world."[15] Dussinger makes a parallel observation when he states that, while Frankenstein "experiences evil from within as a daemonic force, the monster experiences evil from without as social injustice."[16] Critics who have recognized the importance of the doppelgänger theme are tracking inwards while those who connect the monster with technology, like those who connect it with the forces of social revolution, are tracking outwards. Wilfred Cude is perhaps more sensitive to the true nature of this outward direction when he identifies the monster more generally with the dangers of scientific creativity.[17] But the French Revolution *is* a factor in *Frankenstein* and technology, a revolutionary force, may certainly be comprehended in retrospect as an aspect of human reality. And technology, like any other product of a "fallen" human knowledge, might justifiably be regarded as destructive. My basic point, of course, is that the construction of *Frankenstein* is specifically designed to allow for the possibility that the outward and the inward, the centripetal and the centrifugal, are mirror images of one another, or otherwise in collusion.

97

The gamut of identifications for which I am arguing may be indirectly corroborated by Mary Shelley's revealing use of the word "progeny" to describe her book and the shape of human knowledge in a way that links both with the monster. Towards the end of her Introduction, Mary makes the following statement regarding her book: "I bid my hideous progeny go forth and prosper" (p. 10). This is as clear an indication as one could wish that Mary saw her book and the monster in terms of one another. It conjures up Frankenstein's less welcome fantasy of the monster and his potential mate going forth and propagating "a race of devils" (p. 165). In the body of *Frankenstein*, to reiterate that suggestive phrase, the image of progeny is applied to a branch of knowledge. For a brief period, on hearing about electricity, Frankenstein is persuaded to dismiss the works of the alchemists: "I at once gave up my former occupations; set down natural history and its progeny as a deformed and abortive creation; and entertained the greatest disdain for a would-be science, which could never even step within the threshold of real knowledge" (p. 41). But since this resolution is short-lived, it seems that Frankenstein did come to identify the deformed, abortive creation of natural history and its progeny with "real knowledge." The overall effect of the image is, clearly, to equate the deformed, abortive shape of human knowledge with the deformed, abortive shape of Frankenstein's creation. Indeed, the monster speaks of himself as "an abortion, to be spurned at, and kicked, and trampled on" (p. 222).

As the shape of human reality, human knowledge, characteristics other than the monster's outlandish size should be taken into account; specifically a certain vagueness about his form and the overwhelming impression that that form is misshapen, ugly. Mary's point seems to be that the reality constituted by human knowledge is fallen and therefore unpleasant to behold. But it is not fallen in any conventional Christian sense. It is fallen because we cannot fully know what we think we know. The nature of human knowledge is radically uncertain and largely metaphoric if we cannot decide whether what we "know" exists inside or outside the mind of man. Hence its vagueness of outline. As Frankenstein momentarily recognizes, "It seemed to me as if nothing would or could ever be known" (p. 41). This state of affairs is imaged in the Christian terms of the Fall but should be understood only in terms of the equation presented between knowledge and imperfection. Early on, Frankenstein warns Walton, "You seek for knowledge and wisdom, as I once did; and I ardently hope that the gratification of your wishes may not be a serpent to sting you, as mine has been" (pp. 29-30). The monster identifies himself with the Fall when he tells Frankenstein, "I will watch with the wiliness of a snake, that I may sting with its venom" (p. 168). And sure

98

enough, Frankenstein finds that he has been stung. His hopes of happiness with Elizabeth—the knowledge of love—have been undermined by the monster's threat: "I read and reread her letter, and some softened feelings stole into my heart, and dared to whisper paradisiacal dreams of love and joy; but the apple was already eaten, and the angel's arm bared to drive me from all hope" (p. 189).

The central portion of the book is given over to the monster's quest for and acquisition of knowledge, a knowledge which is finally synonymous with doubt. His liberal arts education, which depends fundamentally on a knowledge of language, occurs in an enclosed, quasi-Edenic context. The three "set" books that he reads, *The Sorrows of Werther*, Plutarch's *Lives* and *Paradise Lost*, provide a sequential sense of the relationships between the human microcosm and the cosmic macrocosm; a sense of pitiful personal history comprehended within a larger historical and social framework, and both finally dwarfed by an enveloping metaphysical reality. The monster can be related to all three contexts but he comes personally to favour himself in the role of Milton's Satan, a role signifying in Mary Shelley's terms a state fallen because uncertain.

Arriving previously at a dawning self-knowledge, the monster twice refers to himself as a blot. But in each case the sense of the word is different and it is a combination of the two senses which best defines his "Satanic" role. In the first case, he sees himself as a stain, like original sin: "Was I . . . a blot upon the earth, from which all men fled, and whom all men disowned?" (p. 120). But two paragraphs down he is using the same word to mean something not known: "all my past life was now a blot, a blind vacancy in which I distinguished nothing" (p. 121). Likewise, our "knowledge" of human reality is a blot; it is fallen or imperfect because it masks a void. No wonder the monster exclaims, "Of what a strange nature is knowledge! It clings to the mind, when it has once seized on it, like lichen on the rock" (p. 120). Is it a psychosomatic disease of the mind or is it a matter of external contagion? Is the monster genuinely external, genuinely Other, or is he a scapegoat projection? This dilemma is the source of the monster's agony: "What was I? The question again recurred, to be answered only with groans" (p. 121).

What makes knowledge so difficult to pin down is its protean character. It changes with time and hence again the appropriateness of the Christian analogy as rationalistically interpreted. The Bible equates the acquisition of knowledge with the fall into time. I have detailed evidence linking the monster with reality as understood in the "external," spatial terms of sea, moon and mountains. Equally, the monster directly relates himself to the human experience of temporal process. We return here to the two occasions when the monster refers to "the series of my being" (pp. 219, 222), a phrase that may owe something to Locke's claim that man derives his notion of time or duration from reflection on the "train of *Ideas*, which constantly succeed one another in his Understanding, as long as he is awake."[18] L. J. Swingle is on to one of the meanings of this semantically loaded phrase when he observes that the monster cannot be fully known because he is not something static; rather he is in the process of becoming.[19] In the context of what I believe to be Mary Shelley's intention, the phrase implies that human reality also is time-bound, in the process of becoming and therefore finally unknowable.

The observation of change in *Frankenstein* provides the most painful recognition of man's fallen, time-conditioned state. Thus, the melancholy nature of Frankenstein's reflections, when returning to Geneva after an absence of six years, has to do with more than William's death: "How altered everything might be during that time! One sudden and desolating change had taken place; but a thousand little circumstances might have by degrees worked other alterations, which, although they were done more tranquilly, might not be the less decisive" (p. 74). Disturbed emotions are an inevitable response to a reality whose uncertainty has much to do with its changeability: "Naught may endure but mutability" (p. 98) is the resigned conclusion of the extract from Shelley's "On Mutability," a poem which reflects Frankenstein's mood in the face of the inexorably moving glacier a moment before the confrontation with the monster. A similar confusion characterizes the monster's mixed reactions to a scene inside the cottage symbolizing the dialectic of age and youth. A young girl is sitting beside an old man. In response to a mournful tune, which he plays on an instrument the monster cannot identify, she weeps and kneels at his feet. He comforts her. As for the monster: "I felt sensations of a peculiar and over-powering nature: they were a mixture of pain and pleasure, such as I had never before experienced, either from hunger or cold, warmth or food; and I withdrew from the window, unable to bear these emotions" (p. 108).

A total appreciation of the radical uncertainty of the nature of human knowledge and reality may well hit an intellectual innocent in such a manner as to occasion what might be called a "philosophical apocalypse."[20] Following Justine's execution for the murder of William, "vice and injustice" (p. 92), previously confined in Elizabeth's experience to the realm of fiction, invade reality. Her assumptions have been overturned and now she does not know what to think. Justine, whom she believed to be (like herself) good and innocent, has been found guilty and nothing is the same any more: "Alas! Victor, when falsehood can look so like truth, who can assure themselves of certain happiness? I feel as if I were walking the edge of a precipice, towards which thousands are crowding and endeavouring to plunge me into the abyss" (p. 93). But, as L. J. Swingle shrewdly notes, Elizabeth does not abide by this intuition. She steps back from the abyss and "knows" that Justine is innocent. Thus she defines herself as an innocent and potential victim. The monster destroys Innocents.[21] Or, in the terms for which I am arguing, it is human reality which destroys Innocents.

Justine's trial is the first of what appears to be a series of unjust trials in *Frankenstein*. The mechanism of a trial clearly bears on the problematic ontological state that *Frankenstein* as a whole explores. Contradictory evidence is brought forward, weighed and a verdict is rendered. There can be no guarantees that the final verdict will coincide with the truth of the case that is being tried. In the four trials described in the book, the conclusions arrived at by the process of justice appear not to coincide with what appears to be the truth. Apparently, Justine is wrongly convicted. Her name, a plea for justice, seems to be a cruel irony. In this respect, it belongs with two other Christian names in the story: Felix and Victor.

Safie's father "was tried and condemned to death" in Paris on an apparently trumped-up charge; again justice is seemingly travestied although, as I have previously noted, this may not be the case: "The injustice of this sentence was very flagrant; all Paris was indignant; and it was judged that his religion and wealth, rather than the crime alleged against him, had been the cause of his condemnation" (p. 122). As a result of helping Safie's father escape, Felix finds himself on trial. The guilty verdict and the punishment—exile and confiscation of wealth—is technically just, but monstrously unjust by any human standards. The fourth trial is Frankenstein's and takes place in Ireland. His is the only trial that results in a not guilty verdict. It is found that he did not murder Clerval. But, if the monster is Frankenstein's doppelgänger, then surely Frankenstein is guilty?

It is clearly intended that the reader apply the concept of a trial, in something like a Kafkaesque sense, to the entire novel. The monster recognizes that, when he makes his presence known to the cottagers, he must expect some form of judgement and attempts to fortify himself "for the trial which in a few months [he] resolved to undergo" (p. 131). He makes initial overtures to the blind old man and, hearing the approach of the old man's sighted children and Safie, the monster exclaims ineffectually: "Do not you desert me in the hour of trial!" (p. 135). Life becomes as much a trial, an ordeal, for Frankenstein as for his monster, especially in view of the monster's threat: " *'I will be with you on your wedding night!'* Such was my sentence" (p.

188), Frankenstein legalistically adds. A surgeon will later pronounce the "sentence" (p. 216) of Frankenstein's imminent death.

But just as insistent is the monster's cry for justice: "Oh, Frankenstein, be not equitable to every other, and trample upon me alone, to whom thy justice, and even thy clemency and affection, is most due" (p. 100); "on you only had I any claim for pity and redress, and from you I determined to seek that justice which I vainly attempted to gain from any other being that wore the human form" (p. 139). The monster, claiming (in the Godwinian accents of an ideal social benevolence as expressed in *Political Justice*) that his evil actions are a consequence of "a forced solitude" (p. 147), persuades Frankenstein that "the justice due both to him and to my fellow creatures demanded of me that I should comply with his request" (p. 148) for an equally grotesque mate, in the monster's words, "as hideous as myself" (p. 145). He requires, as we have noted, a mirror image. Later, Walton comes to feel that "in justice" (p. 214) he could not refuse the sailor's insistence that, if the ship is freed from the ice, it should head for home. Thwarted in his aspirations, Walton does return but "It requires more philosophy than I possess, to bear this injustice with patience" (p. 215). And the monster too, as he explains to Walton, rankles at the way in which his desire for fellowship was spurned: "Was there no injustice in this? (p. 221). He instances Felix's violent rejection: "Even now my blood boils at the recollection of this injustice" (p. 222).

It appears that the trial of life in *Frankenstein* is synonymous with injustice. The "facts" of a case are seemingly irrelevant, not because such "facts" may not exist but because they simply cannot be apprehended given the contingent human state. The reader of *Frankenstein* is put in a position of judging the evidence of three narrators each bearing witness to his own experience, the "facts" as he chooses to see them. Like Faulkner and many other writers, Mary is using the technique of multiple first-person narration to dramatize the relativity of reality. But unlike most of Faulkner's narrators, Mary Shelley's do not have an equal ontological existence in the world of *Frankenstein*. Of the two key participants, we are told that one is dead and that the other plans to immolate himself. In spite of the illusion of first person narration, Frankenstein's account is once removed and the monster's story is twice removed from "actuality." One effect of the regressive Chinese box structure is the illusionistic sense of a disappearing series. The jury-member reader has only the documentary evidence of Walton's letters and the written record that he has made of Frankenstein's narrative, "as nearly as possible in his own words" (p. 30), including Frankenstein's recollection of what the monster told him. While Walton made his record each night of what he

102

heard Frankenstein relate during the day, Frankenstein did not make any kind of written record of the monster's history. If that history is to be taken literally, it can only be on the basis of a narrative convention so strained as to highlight the violation of "reality" that such conventions are designed to circumvent. But on a word by word basis, that central portion of the book has to be largely a fabrication. Unless, of course, the monster is Frankenstein.

And if the monster is an aspect of Frankenstein why should not both be aspects of Walton? After all, he is the only survivor. Is it possible, then, that the world of Frankenstein exists only within Walton's head? This would be one way of explaining the monster's survival after Frankenstein's "death." Is there a line to be drawn between what is happening within Walton's head and what is happening outside? One critic has suggested that the aura of ontological uncertainty in Shakespeare's *The Tempest* invites the speculation that all that transpires is an anxiety dream, experienced by Prospero in his library in Milan, warning him about the dangers of neglecting his royal responsibilities.[22] Equally it might be argued that the substance of *Frankenstein* is an anxiety dream on Walton's part. Before the "dream" commences, Walton is acutely conscious of his need for companionship and the result of the "dream" is his return to England and his beloved sister. While such speculation is encouraged by the text it can in no way be verified.

Understandably the monster is aware of the dubious status of his own narrative and his own reality. Consequently, he twice draws attention to the existence of corroborative documentary evidence. His knowledge of Safie's background comes, he claims, from reading her letters to Felix. He made "copies of these letters" and tells Frankenstein, "Before I depart, I will give them to you, they will prove the truth of my tale . . ." (p. 123). Later on, the monster has occasion to refer to and actually give Frankenstein an additional piece of evidence, the papers he discovered in "the pocket of the dress which I had taken from your laboratory:" "It was your journal of the four months that preceded my creation" (p. 130).

Clearly, the monster wants to know the truth and he wants to be believed. But in the context of *Frankenstein* it is not possible to know the truth about anything. And the reader should be particularly suspicious about the monster's final statements concerning his plans to immolate himself. We do not see him do it. He only says that he will do it. Perhaps he is lying. In the concluding sentence he is lost in the "darkness and distance" of futurity. There is something very end-of-the-world about this projected "conflagration" (p. 223) which completes a scenario Walton describes as "this final and wonderful catastrophe" (p. 218). The word "conflagration" better describes a world in flames than a single individual in flames. But, then, as I have argued, there

103

is much in the book to suggest that the monster is the metaphoric world of human reality.

Thus, *The Last Man*, which Mary began writing six years after the publication of *Frankenstein*, is implicit in the apocalypse that the monster foresees. In the later book, Lionel Verney, Mary Shelley's persona, awakes from a dream which Brian Aldiss rightly compares with Frankenstein's horrific dream:[23]

> Methought I had been invited to Timon's last feast; I came with keen appetite, the covers were removed, the hot water sent up its satisfying steams, while I fled before the anger of the host, who assumed the form of Raymond; while to my diseased fancy, the vessels hurled by him after me were surcharged with fetid vapour, and my friend's shape, altered by a thousand distortions, expanded into a gigantic phantom, bearing on its brow the sign of pestilence. The growing shadow rose and rose, filling, and then seeming to endeavour to burst beyond, the adamantine vault that bent over, sustaining and enclosing the world.[24]

Raymond here is based on Byron, but the image of a figure distorted into a ballooning gigantic "phantom" and finally coinciding with an enclosed, "adamantine" world of human reality accords well with the possible reality of the monster who is twice discovered "bent over" the body of Frankenstein. The plague in *The Last Man* might be regarded as a metaphor for the "fallen" reality of *Frankenstein* as evidenced by the destructive enroachment of the suspicion of solipsism upon the structure of human knowledge. *The Last Man* clearly implies that for Mary Shelley the death of her husband was the end of the world. She must have lived with the uncomfortable intuition that she existed only within the solipsistic world "created" by another being.

But *Frankenstein* is patently open-ended. Whatever resolution may be projected lies beyond the bounds of that fictional world. The final image of a figure "lost in darkness and distance" (p. 223) is of a figure engulfed by the unknown. And such a figure dramatizes the reader's predicament. Unlike Shelley, Mary has no philosophical answers. What she presents in *Frankenstein*, at the cost of a certain narrative incoherence, is a spectrum of possibilities. This philosophical spectrum has a certain abstract order which holds together whatever else may appear contradictory and disorganized. *Frankenstein* is best understood in terms of a philosophical appreciation of the sliding relationships between the Self and the Other. Consideration of both these elements provokes unease. The extreme possibility that nothing exists outside the Self perverts and renders meaningless both knowledge and love. The Other is alarming precisely because it is the Other, the unknown and the threatening. But knowledge, in any real sense, depends upon the existence and identification of that Other.

In *Frankenstein*, four possible aspects or areas of the Other are identified. First, there is the existence of other human beings: relations, lovers, friends and society at large. Secondly, there is the external universe of nature: trees sea, mountains, moon and stars. This universe presumably includes all forms of life other than man, both animal and vegetable. The monster is, of course, presented as the prime example of what may be the Other; he exists beyond the pale of humanity and nature. In this listing he is primarily but not exclusively the third instance of the Other. The possibility of a transcendental reality accounts for the final and ultimate area which may be categorzied as Other. However, the overall function of the monster is to encompass this fourfold Otherness: at different times he takes on characteristics of the sexual Other and the revolutionary Other, the environmental Other and the transcendental Other.

What is confusing and open-ended in *Frankenstein* results from an inability to be confident about these divisions. They constantly appear to overlap and obliterate one another. If Frankenstein's search for "the secrets of heaven and earth" (p. 37) is to be successful, he must be certain that he has established the limits of the Self. This is why, in searching for the secret of life and creating an artificial being, he needs to tap the *spiritual* power of electricity. Actually it might equally be argued that what Frankenstein is most fascinated by and most desires for himself is death since death is assumed to be the immediate prelude to eternal spiritual life—hence Frankenstein's efforts to create life involve much time spent in the charnel house. Nevertheless, because life is identified with a spiritual power, it follows that the creation of life does demonstrate the existence of a trancendental Other. The existence of a transcendental reality represents the ultimate hope of something beyond the Self. In *Melincourt*, Thomas Love Peacock, a friend of both the Shelleys, defines transcendentalism as the "discovery of the difference between *objective* and *subjective* reality."[25] Certainly, all other manifestations of the Other in *Frankenstein* are radically questioned. The people whom one "loves" may exist only as projections of the self. If the monster is actually another projection, Frankenstein's doppelgänger, then it is Frankenstein himself who murders William, Clerval and Elizabeth. But equally, both murderer and victims, together with the external universe, may be aspects of Frankenstein's mind, or Walton's mind. The possible permutations are endless.

The intermediate plasticity of reality is shown to be at one with the intermediate ontological status of the monster. Likewise the configuration of elements that coalesced in Mary's head to produce her monstrous creation

105

Frankenstein is an indeterminate mix or nexus of the "external" and "internal." This in-between state, as indicated in Chapter 4, well describes the mechanics of metaphor and it is itself the matrix of metaphor. Thus, the book, the monster and human reality are metaphors of one another. This identity owes something to the extent that all metaphor involves the confusion of the human and the non-human; a metaphoric condition is inherently monstrous.

It must be admitted that the ontology implied by the concluding paragraph of *Frankenstein* is not particularly encouraging. The sense of aloneness is overwhelming and solitude is a necessary adjunct of solipsism.[26] The "blackness" and "distance" which surrounds and engulfs the monster (which may be taken as surrounding and engulfing human reality) looks suspiciously like a void, Locke's *tabula rasa* not externalized but actual. The transcendent in *Frankenstein* is suspiciously allied with the relationship between natural phenomena and human cognition. If the sublime experience is to be explained in terms of the mechanism of sublimation, then the possibility must be faced that what is assumed to be a transcendental Otherness may be, like all other aspects of reality, an anthropomorphic projection. But this is in no way to deny the "reality" of what comes across to every reader of Mary Shelley's novel: the "fact" that a man named Frankenstein, having discovered the secret of life and death, *does* succeed in creating a living being.

APPENDIX: THE PREFERRED TEXT?

Mary's *Journal* entry for May 14, 1817, includes the statement, "Shelley . . . corrects 'Frankenstein,' "[1] On the basis of these corrections, which are presumably the ones that appear in the extant manuscript fragments and constitute the only hard evidence for assessing Shelley's portion of the published text, James Rieger asks: "Should we grant him the status of minor collaborator?"[2] My answer is no. It is true that Shelley did contribute some sentences and phrases; accordingly in the previous pages, wherever a supportive quotation derives in part from Shelley I have mentioned the fact. But none of these additions, including the longest—the four consecutive sentences beginning "The republican institutions of our country . . . " (p. 65)[3] can be counted as truly substantial. Most of the time, as in the case of the sample manuscript sheet reproduced following this page and the other sheets reproduced earlier, Shelley confines himself to changing a word or smoothing a stylistic inelegance. To judge from a letter to the publisher, dated October 22, 1817, Shelley saw his role as that of an editor: "I have paid considerable attention to the correction of such few instances of baldness of style as necessarily occur in the production of a very young writer. . . . "[4]

Occasionally, Shelley's changes, as evident from the manuscript fragments, do draw attention to problematic areas. At one weak point in the narrative logic, Mary is required to explain why Frankenstein, in spite of the monster's threat to be with him on his wedding night, decides not to delay his marriage. She originally wrote of the marriage, "It might indeed hasten ["my fate" by] a few months but if he suspected that I delayed on his account he would certainly revenge himself some other way." Shelley's version, which Mary adopted in both the 1818 and 1831 texts, presents the same weak argument: "My destruction might indeed arrive a few months sooner; but if my torturer should suspect that I postponed it, influenced by his menaces, he would surely find other, and perhaps more dreadful means of revenge" (p. 189). Presumably Shelley changed Mary's original because he recognized its fatuousness, but that fatuousness is still there in his sentence. Perhaps the words "destructive," "torturer," "menaces" and "dreadful" elicit an emotional reaction which serves to distract attention from whatever rationalistic objections might be raised. But it is equally true that Shelley's heightening focusses attention on a sentence that might otherwise slip by. Of course, the weakness of the excuse and the fact that neither Mary nor Shelley raise the possibility of Frankenstein's preparing to take defensive action against the monster (some

fulfil my pilgrimage without — them — I should
have sunk under my hardships. but during the day
I was sustained & inspirit-
ted by the hope of night, — for in sleep I saw
my friend my wife & my beloved country
again I saw the benevolent countenance
of my father, — heard the silver tones of
my Elizabeth voice and beheld Herbal
enjoying health & youth — often when
wearied by a toilsome march I persua-
did myself that I was then dreaming &
that [ ] I enjoyed reality when I [ ] again
in the arms of my dearest friends [ ] what
agonizing fondness did I feel for [ ]
did I cling to their dear forms as [ ]
my [ ] as wakened [ ] and per
suade myself that they still lived [ ]
moments the vengeance that burned
within me died in my heart, and thenceforward
my path towards the destruction of the devil more as a task enjoined by heaven,
than the ardent desire of my soul
[ ] his feelings were whom Ither
I [ ] know but sometimes indeed he
left marks in writing on the bark of
trees or cut on stone that guided me,
& instigated my fury — my reign is not yet
over, he said on one of these inscriptions you live &
my power is complete. follow me — I seek
the everlasting ices of the north where you
will feel the misery of [ ] cold & frost which
[ ] [ ] [ ] sweeter to me
[ ] you will find near this place
if you follow not too tardily, a dead hair
[ ] & be avenged — food some on my enemy

such preparation would have made the decision to go ahead with the marriage more reasonable) may indicate that Frankenstein actually seeks self-destruction. Nevertheless, whether this "revealing" ambiguity, if intentional, is best couched in Mary's economically flattened terms or Shelley's more expansive phraseology is still open to question.

Rieger's account of Shelley's changes contains several inaccuracies. For example, he asserts that "it was Shelley's idea that Frankenstein journey to England for the purpose of creating a female monster."[5] A manuscript annotation, that Rieger presumably misread, indicates that Shelley had thoughts only about who should propose the journey to England: "I think the journey to England ought to be Victor's proposal—that he ought to go for the purpose of collecting knowledge, thro the promotion of a remark he ought to lead his father to this in the conversation—the conversation commences right enough." This suggestion is difficult to read and, given that Rieger was working not from the original manuscript but with a print from the microfilm of Lord Abinger's collection,[6] his erroneous interpretation is understandable. But a further misstatement of fact is particularly puzzling. Rieger writes, "Most important of all, Shelley revised the ending from the last paragraph of Frankenstein's dying speech . . . to the Monster's disappearance in darkness and distance."[7] These pages of the manuscript contain only one indication of Shelley's hand, the addition, "such as you cannot even imagine" (p. 220).[8]

Without Shelley Mary might not have developed her idea to novel length but the way in which the story progresses and the implications drawn from that progression seem to be attributable solely to her authorship. I see no reason to join Rieger in questioning her claim in the Introduction she wrote for the 1831 edition that "I certainly did not owe the suggestion of one incident, nor scarcely of one train of feeling, to my husband" (p. 10). Equally, my analysis in Chapter 4 of the relationship between Shelley's "Mont Blanc" and some of the Alpine description in both the 1818 and 1831 versions of *Frankenstein* indicates that there is no compulsion to follow Rieger's conclusion that Mary "virtually plagiarizes the diction, ideas, and symbolism of Shelley's" poem.[9] It seems less a case of Mary appropriating metaphors that "Shelley coined"[10] than of a similar reaction to a shared experience. Of course, there is much in *Frankenstein* to be explained with regard to Mary's knowledge of Shelley himself and the general philosophical and literary education that he must have given her. But it was not a case of uncritical acceptance. Just as Frankenstein may be regarded as a critical portrait of Shelley the man, any body of ideas that she may have derived from him is placed in a revisionary or skeptical context. Mary Shelley deserves all the credit she has received as the authoress of *Frankenstein*. It was to no degree a case of dual authorship and consequently the argument for preferring the 1818 version because it preserves the integrity of a joint vision is specious.

Undoubtedly, Rieger's attempt to question the authority of the 1831 edition has more to do with justifying his reissue of the 1818 text than with any elasticity in the facts of authorship. However, there are significant, circumstantial differences between the two editions and that fact alone is sufficient justification for making the 1818 edition generally available.[11] Irrespective of the authorial issue, a case might be made for preferring the original version. Although Rieger's edition includes a valuable full collation of the two texts, he does not make out such a case beyond maintaining "that on balance Mary Shelley's changes were slightly for the worse. . . . "[12] Again I must disagree, both with his judgement and with Rieger's claim that Mary's statement about those changes in her 1831 Introduction is, not to put too fine an edge on it, misleading. Rieger quotes out of context Mary's statement, "I have changed no portion of the story, nor introduced any new ideas or circumstances" (p. 10). The surrounding sentences indicate that, while most of the changes are stylistic, there are others which "are entirely confined to such parts as are mere adjuncts to the story, leaving the core and substance of it untouched" (p. 11). Taken in its entirety, this account of Mary's alterations is accurate.

The stylistic changes are mainly in the interests of clarity, economy and grammatical impact. As for the "major" changes (for example, the introduction of Elizabeth as unrelated to Frankenstein, the presentation of Frankenstein's father as non-scientific, and having Frankenstein journey to Chamonix unaccompanied by Elizabeth and his father), I have drawn attention to most of them in the course of this study and explained why I think they are improvements. For the present it will be sufficient to examine one instance: the episode in which the monster "plants" on Justine's person the miniature of Frankenstein's mother that he has taken from the murdered William. In the unlikely sequence of the 1818 edition, the monster, having seen Justine walking about, "aproached her unperceived, and placed the portrait securely in one of the folds of her dress."[13] In her account of how she came to be wandering around, Justine mentions being "Unable to rest or sleep."[14] In the revised version, "towards morning she believed that she slept for a few minutes" (p. 83) until disturbed by some steps. And in the revised version of the monster's account, it transpires that he placed the incriminating evidence while Justine "was sleeping on some straw" (p. 143). There can be no question that here the 1831 edition is more credible than and therefore an improvement on that of 1818. This improvement is, I believe, representative and, thus, we may feel some assurance in concluding that the authoritative text of *Frankenstein* is also the superior one.

NOTES

NOTES TO CHAPTER 1

[1] See the Preface to *The Tragic Muse* in the "New York Edition" of *The Novels and Tales of Henry James* (New York: Charles Scribner's Sons, 1936), VII, x.

[2] See, particularly *Anatomy of Criticism* (Prinecton, N.J.: Princeton University Press, 1957) and *The Secular Scripture: A Study of the Structure of Romance* (Cambridge, Mass.: Harvard University Press, 1976).

[3] See "*Frankenstein* and the Tradition of Realism," *Novel*, 7 (Fall, 1973), 24.

[4] Anybody upset by the fact that I frequently refer to Mary Shelley by her Christian name only, yet never identify her husband simply as Percy, will likely not be assuaged by whatever explanation I have to offer. However, I am persuaded by the rationale that, although the convention which I am following may be a patronizing one, it has the overriding advantages of clarity and convenience.

[5] *Quarterly Review*, 36 (January, 1818), 382.

[6] Quoted in Howard B. Gotlieb, *William Beckford of Fonthill* (New Haven: Yale University Press, 1969), p. 61.

[7] Letter to Mrs. Marshall, dated November 15, 1822, reproduced in Julian Marshall, *The Life and Letters of Mary Wollstonecraft Shelley* (London: Richard Bentley & Son, 1888), II, 52.

[8] All parenthetical page references within my text are to the 1831 edition of *Frankenstein; or, The Modern Prometheus*, ed. M. K. Joseph (London: Oxford University Press, 1969).

[9] See " 'My Accursed Origin': The Search for the Mother in *Frankenstein*," *Studies in Romanticism*, 15 (Spring, 1976), 172-74.

NOTES TO CHAPTER 2

[1] Harold Bloom makes the point that "*Frankenstein* affords a unique introduction to the archetypal world of the Romantics" in a twice republished essay that is most conveniently available as an Afterword to the Signet Classic edition of *Frankenstein* (New York: New American Library, 1965), p. 215. See also the unpublished dissertation by Cecily M. Callaghan, "Mary Shelley and *Frankenstein*: A Compendium of Romanticism," Leland Stanford Junior University, 1936.

² See, for example, R. J. Z. Werblowsky, *Lucifer and Prometheus: A Study of Milton's Satan* (London: Routledge and Kegan Paul, Ltd., 1952).

³ See *Mary Shelley's Journal*, ed. Frederick L. Jones (Norman: University of Oklahoma Press, 1944), pp. 43-47.

⁴ See Dryden's translation of Book I, 11. 101-12, of the *Metamorphoses* in *The Works of John Dryden*, ed. A. B. Chambers and William Frost (Berkeley: University of California Press, 1974), IV, 378-79.

⁵ This leads Christopher Small to the hypothesis that Frankenstein was prevented by precedent from creating a female mate for his monster. See Small's *Ariel Like a Harp: Shelley, Mary and "Frankenstein"* (London: Gollancz, 1972), published in the U.S.A. with the same pagination but the weaker title *Mary Shelley's "Frankenstein": Tracing the Myth* (Pittsburgh: University of Pittsburgh Press, 1973), p. 50.

⁶ *Mary Shelley's Journal*, pp. 53, 61.

⁷ "Philosophical and Literary Sources of *Frankenstein*," *Comparative Literature*, 17 (Spring, 1965), 101.

⁸ "Pecksie," "Maie" and "Dormouse" were among Shelley's nicknames for Mary. See R. Glynn Grylls, *Mary Shelley: A Biography* (London: Oxford University Press, 1938), p. 49, n. 1.

⁹ See The New Mermaids *Friar Bacon and Friar Bungay*, ed. J. A. Lavin (London: Ernest Benn Ltd., 1969), sc. 11, ll. 24-26, p. 14.

¹⁰ See the Revel Plays *Doctor Faustus*, ed. John D. Jump (Methuen & Co., Ltd.: London, 1962), p. 103.

¹¹ For this translation of *Inferno*, XXVI, 118-20, see *Frankenstein; or, The Modern Prometheus* (The 1818 Text), ed. James Rieger (Indianapolis and New York: The Bobbs-Merrill Company, Inc., 1974), p. 212, n. 2.

¹² *Ibid.*, p. 145.

¹³ See Radu Florescu, *In Search of Frankenstein* (Boston: New York Graphic Society, 1975), p. 107. Oddly, Florescu reproduces the error he has corrected when he refers to the Villa Diodati as the place "where, as we have noted, Milton may have stayed during his Italian journey in 1639" (p. 178).

¹⁴ See "List of Books read in 1815" and entries for November 15-22, 1816, pp. 48, 68-69.

¹⁵ *Paradise Lost*, XII, 646.

¹⁶ *Ibid.*, IV, 75, IX, 467.

¹⁷ See *Mary Shelley's Monster, The Story of "Frankenstein"* (Boston: Houghton Mifflin Co., 1976), pp. 68-81; and also Leslie Tannenbaum, "From Filthy Type to Truth: Miltonic Myth in *Frankenstein*," *Keats-Shelley Journal*, 26 (1977), 101-13.

¹⁸ See, for example, Milton A. Mays, "*Frankenstein*, Mary Shelley's Black Theodacy," *Southern Humanities Review*, 3 (Spring, 1969), 146-53;

reprinted in SF: *The Other Side of Realism*, ed. Thomas D. Clareson (Bowling Green, Ohio: Bowling Green University Press, 1971), pp. 171-80.

[19] See entries for September 20 to November 30, 1816, *Mary Shelley's Journal*, pp. 64-70.

[20] "Remarks on *Frankenstein, Or, The Modern Prometheus*, a Novel," *Blackwood's Edinburgh Magazine*, 2 (March, 1818), 619.

[21] See *Billion Year Spree: The True History of Science Fiction*, New York: Doubleday & Co., Inc., 1973; published in the U.K. with an amended subtitle—the "True" is missing—but the same pagination (London: Weidenfeld and Nicolson, 1974), p. 26.

[22] In a letter to Hogg, dated July 28, 1811, Shelley mentions Darwin with approval. He does not say which work he is studying but Jones suggests *The Botanic Garden* as most likely. See *The Letters of Percy Bysshe Shelley*, p. 129 and n. 5. In letters dated December 17, 1812 (p. 342) and December 24, 1812 (p. 245), Shelley orders Darwin's *Zoonomia* and *Temple of Nature* (1803) respectively. For Darwin's influence on Shelley, see Carl Grabo, *A Newton Among Poets* (Chapel Hill: University of North Carolina Press, 1930), pp. 30-79.

[23] See entries for October 28 and 29, 1816, *Mary Shelley's Journal*, p. 67, and Jones's suggested title correction, p. 73.

[24] *Mary Shelley's Journal*, pp. 68-71, 74.

[25] See letter to Leigh Hunt, dated April 8, 1825, in *The Letters of Mary W. Shelley* (Norman: University of Oklahoma Press, 1944), I, 318.

[26] Quoted by M. K. Joseph in Appendix B, "Shaftesbury on Prometheus" in his edition of *Frankenstein*, pp. 228-29. See also the chapter on Mary's "Image of Prometheus" in Christian Kreutz, *Das Prometheussymbol in der Dichtung der englischen Romantic, Palaestra Bd.*, 236 (Goettingen: Vandenhoeck & Ruprecht, 1963), pp. 136-52. This discussion of *Frankenstein's* sources also mentions Shaftesbury's *The Moralists* and Ovid's *Metamorphoses*. But particular attention is given to Francis Bacon's essay "Prometheus, or the State of Man" (1609). I am grateful to Darko Suvin for drawing my attention to Kreutz's study.

[27] "Philosophical and Literary Sources of *Frankenstein*," 105.

[28] *Ibid.*, 107. Mention is made of reading Diderot in the August 4, 1816, entry of *Mary Shelley's Journal*, p. 55.

[29] See entries for June 16, 17, and 26, and July 3, 1817, in *Mary Shelley's Journal*, pp. 81-82.

[30] See Hogg, *The Life of Percy Bysshe Shelly* (London: J. M. Dent and Sons, 1933), I, 263.

[31] Cited by Praz, "Introductory Essay," *Three Gothic Novels*, ed. Peter Fairclough (Harmondsworth, Middlesex: Penguin Books Ltd., 1968), p. 30.

[32] See "List of Books read in 1815," 1816 and 1817, and entries for June 27 to July 2, 1817, *Mary Shelley's Journal*, pp. 48, 73, 82 and 89.

[33] "Philosophical and Literary Sources of *Frankenstein*," 101. *Emile* figures in the September 19-20, 1816 entries, *Mary Shelley's Journal*, p. 64.

[34] "The Noble Savage in Mary Shelley's *Frankenstein*," *Notes and Queries*, 190 (June 15, 1946), 248-50.

[35] See entries for September and October, 1814, *Mary Shelley's Journal*, pp. 16-19, 21.

[36] *Ariel Like a Harpy*, pp. 63-64. For the statement in Shelley's review, see *Shelley's Prose, or the Trumpet of a Prophecy*, ed. David Lee Clarke (Albuquerque: University of New Mexico Press, 1954), p. 307.

[37] *Ariel Like a Harpy*, p. 73. Perhaps Mary supplemented her father's ideas with those of her mother. Janet M. Todd argues that the horrifying situation of the monster is analogous to that of a fallen woman who, excluded from family and society becomes an outcast. Such a woman (Jermina) figures in Mary Wollstonecraft's final unfinished novel, *The Wrongs of Woman; or Maria* (1798). On the basis of a number of plot parallels, Janet Todd presents *Maria* as an additional literary source for *Frankenstein* while observing that, when Mary wrote *Frankenstein*, she herself was in the position of a fallen woman. See "Frankenstein's Daughter: Mary Shelley and Mary Wollstonecraft," *Women and Literature*, 4 (Fall, 1976), 18-27.

[38] See entries for September 16, October 19-20, 1814, and "List of Books read in 1816," *Mary Shelley's Journal*, pp. 15, 21, 71.

[39] See *Shelley's Prose, or the Trumpet of a Prophecy*, p. 308.

[40] *St. Leon* is mentioned in entries for October 15 and November 6, 1814, the "List of Books read in 1815," and in the entry for October 9, 1817, *Mary Shelley's Journal*, pp. 21, 24, 48, 84.

[41] "Remarks on *Frankenstein* . . . ," 614.

[42] *Fleetwood* occurs in the "List of Books read in 1815," *Mary Shelley's Journal*, p. 47.

[43] See entry for November 16, 1814, and the "List of Books read in 1814" and 1815, *Mary Shelley's Journal*, pp. 26, 33, 43, 49.

[44] Small develops the comparison between *Wieland* and *Frankenstein*. See *Ariel Like a Harpy*, p. 98.

[45] See "*Wieland* and *Frankenstein*," *American Literature*, 2 (May 1930), 172-73; and *Wieland; or, The Transformation*, ed. Fred Lewis Patee (New York: Hafner Publishing Co., 1958), p. 242.

[46] Prescott, "*Wieland* and *Frankenstein*," 173. For Mary's first reading *Arthur Mervyn*, see entry for July [23—] 26, 1817, *Mary Shelley's Journal*, p. 83.

[47] See entries for November 26-28, 1814, and "List of Books read in 1815," *Mary Shelley's Journal*, pp. 27, 48-49.

[48] The reading of *Zastrozzi* is mentioned in the entry for October 10, 1814, *Mary Shelley's Journal*, p. 19.

[49] *The Romantic Agony*, trans. Angus Davidson, 2nd edition (London: Oxford University Press, 1970), pp. 15-16.

[50] See the Introduction to Rieger's 1818 edition, pp. xxv-xxvi.

[51] *Mary Shelley's Journal*, p. 16.

[52] *Shelley: His Life and Work* (Cambridge, Mass.: Harvard University Press, 1927), I, 55, note 41. *Romantic Tales* figure in the "List of Books read in 1815," *Mary Shelley's Journal*, p. 49.

[53] See *The Diary of Dr. John Wilhem Polidori, 1816, Relating to Byron, Shelley, etc.*, ed. William Rossetti (London: Elkin Matthews, 1911), p. 128.

[54] " 'My Accursed Origin': The Search for the Mother in *Frankenstein*," 185, note 15.

[55] See "List of Books read in 1816," *Mary Shelley's Journal*, p. 72.

[56] *The Poetical Works of Byron*, Cambridge Edition, rev. John F. Glecknor (Boston: Houghton Mifflin Company, 1975), p. 45, stanza LXII.

[57] *Ibid.*, p. 49, stanza XCII.

[58] *Ibid.*, p. 45, stanza LXII.

[59] *The Complete Poetical Works of Percy Bysshe Shelley*, ed. Neville Rogers (Oxford: Oxford University Press, 1975), II, 43.

[60] *Ibid.*, II, 45 (l. 24).

[61] *Ibid.*, II, 48 (l. 158).

[62] *Ibid.*, II, 63 (l. 702).

[63] See Praz, "Introductory Essay," *Three Gothic Novels*, pp. 28-30.

[64] *Moby-Dick*, ed. Harrison Hayford and Herschel Parker (New York: W. W. Norton and Company, Inc., 1967), p. 390.

[65] See John Vernon, "Melville's 'The Bell Tower,' " *Studies in Short Fiction*, 7 (Spring, 1970), 264-76, for a study of the *Frankenstein* connection. For Melville's acquiring *Frankenstein*, see Merton M. Sealts, Jr., *Melville's Reading* (Madison: University of Wisconsin Press, 1966), p. 94.

[66] *In Search of Frankenstein*, pp. 58-63.

[67] Rieger's 1818 edition, p. 31.

[68] *In Search of Frankenstein*, pp. 61-62.

[69] *Mary Shelley's Journal*, p. 13.

[70] See September 2, 1814, entry in *The Journals of Claire Clairmont*, ed. Marion Kingston Stocking (Cambridge, Mass.: Harvard University Press, 1968), p. 35.

[71] Compare Clerval's juxtapositioning of Germany and Switzerland with that in Mary's entry for September 4, 1814: "We leave Mayence at 6 o'clock, and proceed in a little boat to reach the diligence. The banks of Rhine are very fine—rocks and mountains, crowned with lonely castles; but, alas! at their feet are only still towns for ever; yet did the hills half compensate, as in Switzerland the cottages did not pierce into their very recesses but left something to fancy and solitude." See *Mary Shelley's Journal*, p. 13.

[72] Rieger's 1818 edition, pp. 89-90.

[73] *Ibid.*, p. 90.

[74] See entries for August 23-26, 1814, *Mary Shelley's Journal*, p. 11, and *The Journals of Claire Clairmont*, pp. 29-31. Jane's entries for October 9 and 11, 1814 (pp. 49-50), record that Shelley read aloud from Barruel's account of the Illuminati.

[75] "Radical Rhapsody and Romantic Recoil in the Age of Anticipation: A Chapter in the History of SF," *Science-Fiction Studies*, 2 (November, 1974), 262-64. See also George Levine, "*Frankenstein* and the Tradition of Realism," 25. For extended political interpretations, see Judith Weissman, "A Reading of *Frankenstein* as the Complaint of a Political Wife," *Colby Library Quarterly*, 12 (September, 1976), 171-80; and Lee Sterrenburg, "Mary Shelley's Monster: Politics and Psyche in *Frankenstein*," in *The Endurance of "Frankenstein": Essays on Mary Shelley's Novel*, ed. George Levine and U. C. Knoepflmacher (Berkeley: University of California Press, 1979), pp. 143-72. Sterrenburg points out that the metaphor of collective revolutionary monsters occurs in the political polemics of the 1790s.

[76] *Mary Shelley* (New York: Twayne, 1972), pp. 88-94.

[77] "Mary Shelley's Notes to Shelley's Poems and *Frankenstein*," *Studies in Romanticism*, 16 (Summer, 1967), 238-254.

[78] Quoted in Edmund Dowden, *The Life of Percy Shelley* (London: Kegan Paul, Trench & Co., Ltd., 1886), I, 529.

[79] *Ariel Like a Harpy*, p. 101.

[80] *Ibid.*, pp. 122-55 (Chapter 6: "Ariel and Calaban").

[81] *Shelley: The Pursuit* (London: Weidenfeld and Nicolson, 1974), pp. 187-97.

[82] See Newman I. White, *Shelley* (New York: Alfred A. Knopf, 1940), I, 280-81.

[83] If Shelley influenced *Frankenstein*, the reverse may also have been true. Shortly before his death, Shelley experienced an alarming vision of himself strangling Mary. See Holmes, *Shelley: The Pursuit*, p. 727.

[84] *Ariel Like a Harpy*, pp. 148, 169, 176.

[85] See Holmes, *Shelley: The Pursuit*, p. 163.

[86] See R. Glynn Grylls, *Mary Shelley: A Biography*, p. 59. n. 3.

[87] See Ernest J. Lovell, Jr., "Byron and Mary Shelley," *Keats-Shelley Journal*, 2 (January, 1953), 34-49.

[88] See in this general connection, John M. Hill, "*Frankenstein* and the Physiognomy of Desire, *American Imago*, 32 (Winter, 1975), pp. 335-50; Gordon D. Hirsch, "The Monster Was a Lady: On the Psychology of Mary Shelley's *Frankenstein*," *Hartford Studies in Literature*, 7 (number 3, 1975), pp. 116-53; and Susan Harris Smith, "*Frankenstein*: Mary Shelley's Psychic Divisiveness," *Women and Literature*, 5 (Fall, 1977), 42-53.

[89] The significance of this line from *Mathilda*, ed. Elizabeth Nitchie (Chapel Hill: University of North Carolina Press, 1959), is pointed out by Small in *Ariel Like a Harpy*, p. 186.

[90] "Female Gothic: The Monster's Mother," *New York Review of Books* (March 21, 1974), 24-28; reprinted in *Literary Women* (New York: Doubleday & Co., Inc., 1976), pp. 91-99.

[91] The history of Mary's subsequent pregnancies and offspring was also unfortunate. As has been noted, William, born January 24, 1816, died June 7, 1819. Clare, born September 2, 1817, died September 24, 1818. On July 16, 1822, Mary suffered a miscarriage. Only one child, Percy Florence, born November 12, 1819, did not die prematurely.

Any "weakness" may have been as much on Shelley's side as Mary's. An illegitimate child of his, Elna Adelaide Shelley, born in Naples on December 27, 1818, died just over 15 months later. The mother is unknown but Holmes supports the theory first proposed by Ursula Orange in her article "Eliza, Nursemaid to the Shelleys," *Keats-Shelley Memorial Bulletin*, 6 (1955), 24-34, that the other party was the Shelleys' Swiss maid known only by her Christian name Eliza. Holmes also raises the extraordinary possibility that Claire was similarly pregnant by Shelley and suffered a miscarriage on the same day that Elena was born. See *Shelley: The Pursuit*, pp. 465-74, 481-84.

[92] *Mary Shelley's Journal*, p. 41.

[93] *Literary Women*, p. 97.

[94] " 'My Accursed Origin': The Search for the Mother in *Frankenstein*," 169.

[95] *Ibid.*, 177.

[96] *The Diary of Dr. John William Polidori, 1816, Relating to Byron, Shelley, etc.*, p. 128.

[97] *Mary Shelley's Journal*, pp. 18-19.

[98] " 'My Accursed Origin': The Search for the Mother in *Frankenstein*," 183.

NOTES TO CHAPTER 3

[1] Gordon D. Hirsch demonstrates that the creation of the monster is presented as a masturbatory activity. See "The Monster Was a Lady: On the Psychology of Mary Shelley's *Frankenstein*," 126.

² *The Gaping Pig: Literature and Metamorphosis* (Berkeley: University of California Press, 1969), p. 126.

³ See, Wolfgang Iser, *The Implied Reader: Patterns of Communication in Prose from Bunyan to Beckett* (Baltimore: Johns Hopkins University Press, 1974); and Walter J. Ong, s.j., "The Writer's Audience Is Always a Fiction," *PMLA*, 90 (January 1975), 9-21.

⁴ *The Romantic Novel in England* (Cambridge, Mass.: Harvard University Press, 1972), p. 164.

⁵ Richard J. Dunn observes that the novel's structure reinforces the aloneness of the three narrators. See "Narrative Distance in *Frankenstein*," *Studies in the Novel*, 6 (Winter, 1974), 408-17.

⁶ See, in this connection, Masao Miyoshi, *The Divided Self: A Perspective on the Literature of the Double* (New York: New York University Press, 1970); and Carl F. Keppler, *The Literature of the Second Self* (Tucson: University of Arizona Press, 1972).

⁷ *Child of Light: A Reassessment of Mary Wollstonecraft Shelley* (Hadleigh, Essex: Tower Bridge, 1951), pp. 134-37. Muriel Spark sees the monster as Frankenstein's isolated reason. Irving Massey, on the other hand, interprets the monster as Frankenstein's physicality. See *The Gaping Pig*, p. 127. Harold Bloom's formulation suggests a way in which these divergent positions might be combined. He believes that the monster represents the mind and emotions turned outwards not inwards as in his creator's case. The monster is, therefore, more human than Frankenstein although eventually he develops into a daemon of pure consciousness. See the Afterword to the Signet *Frankenstein*, pp. 215-23.

⁸ "Philosophical and Literary Sources of *Frankenstein*," 105, n. 27. See also Charles Schug, "The Romantic Form of Mary Shelley's *Frankenstein*," *Studies in English Literature*, 17 (Autumn, 1977), 613-14.

⁹ For example, Lowry Nelson, Jr., calls *Frankenstein* "a significant fictional model of the mind." See "Night Thoughts on the Gothic Novel," *Yale Review*, 52 (Winter, 1963), 247.

¹⁰ Glynn R. Grylls speculates that John Trelawny was the first to call the monster Frankenstein in a letter to Claire dated November 27, 1869. See *Mary Shelley: A Biography*, p. 319, n. 2; and *The Letters of Edward John Trelawny*, ed. H. Buxton Forman (London: Oxford University Press, 1910), p. 222. However, Grylls is wrong. There are at least two earlier instances. In Chapter 15 of Elizabeth Gaskell's *Mary Barton*, first published in 1847, this sentence occurs: "The actions of the uneducated seem to me typified in those of Frankenstein, that monster of many human qualities, ungifted with a soul, a knowledge of the difference between good and evil." See *Mary Barton* (London: John Lehmann Ltd., 1947), p. 167. *A Supplement to the Oxford English Dictionary* (1972) fails to note the examples from Trelawny and Gaskell but supplies a still earlier case. The entry reads: "**1838** Gladstone in *Murrays Handbk. Sicily* (1864) p. xlvi,

'They [*sc.* mules] really seem like Frankensteins of the animal creation.' "
I am grateful to Patrick Parrinder for drawing my attention to the Gaskell
and Gladstone references.

[11] Masao Miyoshi makes this point in *The Divided Self*, pp. 82-83.

[12] In view of the generic ambivalence of Frankenstein and its quasi-allegorical
character, Angus Fletcher's study of daemonic figures in allegorical literature may be illuminatingly related to the monster. See his *Allegory: The
Theory of a Symbolic Mode* (Ithaca: Cornell University Press, 1964).

[13] *Paradise Lost*, IV. 110.

[14] Small makes something like this point in *Ariel Like a Harpy*, p. 187.

[15] Mary derived this story from Byron's unfinished drama, *The Deformed
Transformed* (1824).

[16] *The Gaping Pig*, p. 129.

[17] *Ibid.*, p. 130.

[18] *Mary Shelley's Monster*, p. 22.

[19] *Ibid.*, p. 27.

[20] *Ibid.*, p. 21.

[21] *Ibid.*, p. 25.

[22] For alternative analyses of most of the details which Tropp considers, see
Morton Kaplan and Robert Kloss, "Fantasy of Paternity and the Doppelgänger: Mary Shelley's *Frankenstein*," *The Unspoken Motive: A Guide to
Psychoanalytic Literary Criticism* (New York: The Free Press, 1973), pp.
119-45; and Joseph Gerhard, "Frankenstein's Dream: The Child as Father
of the Monster," *Hartford Studies in Literature*, 7 (number 3, 1975),
97-115.

NOTES TO CHAPTER 4

[1] See "The Metamorphosis of the Metaphor" in *The Commentator's Despair: The Interpretation of Kafka's "Metamorphosis"* (Port Washington,
N.Y.: Kennikat Press, 1973), pp. 1-31.

[2] *Mountain Gloom and Mountain Glory: The Development of the Aesthetics
of the Infinite* (Ithaca, N.Y.: Cornell University Press, 1959).

[3] *The Sacred Theory of the Earth: Containing an Account of the Original
of the Earth and of All the General Changes Which It Hath Already
Undergone or Is to Undergo, till the Consummation of All Things* (London: Walter Kettilby, 1684). The quotation is taken from the sixth edition
of 1726, I, 188-89.

[4] *Into the Unknown: The Evolution of Science Fiction from Francis Godwin
to H. G. Wells* (Berkeley: University of California Press, 1970), p. 84.

[5] *A Philosophical Enquiry into the Origins of our Ideas of the Sublime and
Beautiful*, ed. J. T. Boulton (London: Routledge & Paul, 1958), p. 57.

[6] *Ibid.*, p. 58.

[7] *Ibid.*, p. 73.

[8] "Remarks on *Frankenstein* . . . ," 617-18.

[9] *The Letters of Percy Bysshe Shelley*, ed. Frederick L. Jones (London: Oxford University Press, 1964), I, 500. Shelley's poetic reaction to another mountain in 1818 is similarly anthropomorphic but also, I suspect, a deliberate and perhaps jocular literalization of an idea that is present only metaphorically in *Frankenstein*:

> Listen, listen Mary mine,
> To the whisper of the Apennine,
> . . . .
> The Apennine in the light of day
> Is a mighty mountain dim and grey
> Which between the earth and sky doth lay;
> But when the night comes, a chaos dread
> On the dim starlight then is spread
> And the Apennine walks abroad with the storm.

See "Passage to the Apennines" in *The Complete Works of Percy Bysshe Shelley*, ed. Roger Ingpen and Walter E. Peck (London: Ernest Benn Ltd., 1926-30), III, 199. A possible source for this fantasy in *Frankenstein* occurs in the context of the boat-stealing episode in *The Prelude*. Wordsworth writes:

> a huge peak, black and huge
> As if with voluntary power instinct,
> Upreared its head. I struck and struck again
> And growing still in stature the grim shape
> Towered up between me and the stars, and still,
> For so it seemed, with purpose of its own
> And measured motion like a living thing,
> Strode after me. (I, 378-85)

Subsequently, Wordsworth records "unknown modes of being" (I, 393) and "huge and mighty forms that do not live / Like living men . . . were a trouble to my dreams" (I, 398-400).

[10] *The Complete Works of Percy Bysshe Shelley*, II, 78-79 (lines 102-106).

[11] See Neville Rogers, Chap. 7, "The Dome. The Eye and the Star. The Philosophic Imagination," *Shelley at Work: A Critical Inquiry*, rev. ed. (London: Oxford University Press, 1967), pp. 105-19.

[12] *The Complete Poetical Works of Percy Bysshe Shelley*, II, 79 (lines 109-111).

[13] *Ibid.*, II, 76 (lines 34-40).

[14] *The Mutiny Within: The Heresies of Percy Bysshe Shelley* (New York: George Braziller, Inc., 1967), pp. 81-89.

[15] *The Romantic Sublime* (Baltimore: Johns Hopkins University Press, 1976), *passim*.

[16] *Mary Shelley's Monster*, pp. 41-47. See also Philmus, *Into the Unknown*, pp. 85-86.

[17] Rieger's 1818 edition, p. 30.

[18] *Mary Shelley dans son oeuvre: Contributions aux études shelleyenes* (Paris: Editions Klincksieck, 1969), p. 350.

[19] See Chapter 2, footnote 23, and Rieger, *The Mutiny Within*, p. 244. For an alternative or additional possibility, see Laura E. Crouch, "Davy's *A Discourse, Introductory to a Course of Lectures on Chemistry*: A Possible Scientific Source of *Frankenstein*," *Keats-Shelley Journal*, 27 (1978), 35-44.

[20] *The Life of Percy Shelley* (London: E. Moxon, 1858), I, 69-70.

[21] *Ibid.*, I, 51.

[22] See "Dr. Polidori and the Genesis of *Frankenstein*," *Studies in English Literature*, 3 (Autumn, 1963), 461-72; reprinted slightly revised in *The Mutiny Within*, pp. 237-47; and *The Diary of Dr. John Polidori 1816, Relating to Byron, Shelley, etc.*, ed. W. M. Rossetti, p. 124.

[23] *The Diary of Dr. John Polidori*, p. 123.

[24] "Dr. Polidori and the Genesis of *Frankenstein*," as in *The Mutiny Within*, p. 243.

[25] Florescu speculates that Mary and Polidori had an affair. See *In Search of Frankenstein*, p. 116.

[26] *Mary Shelley: A Biography*, p. 320. Desmond King-Hele calls *Frankenstein* the "first and most famous work of science fiction." See *Erasmus Darwin* (London: Macmillan, 1963), p. 143. Brian Aldiss makes out an extended case for this proposition in a chapter entitled "The Origins of the Species: Mary Shelley" in *Billion Year Spree*, pp. 7-39. If Mary's original will not quite fit the bill, Aldiss has provided his own more science-fictional version, *Frankenstein Unbound* (London: Faber, 1973). See also Samuel Holmes Vasbinder, "Scientific Attitudes in Mary Shelley's *Frankenstein*: Newtonian Monism as a Base for the Novel," an unpublished (and it must be said unconvincing) dissertation, Kent State University, 1976.

[27] Rieger's 1818 edition, p. 6.

[28] "Remarks on *Frankenstein* . . . ," 614.

[29] "Kinship and Guilt in Mary Shelley's *Frankenstein*," *Studies in the Novel*, 8 (Spring, 1976), 42.

[30] Rieger's 1818 edition, p. 35, n. 8.

[31] Introduction to Rieger's 1818 edition, p. xxvii; quoted in *In Search of Frankenstein*, p. 234.

[32] "Dr. Polidori and the Genesis of *Frankenstein*," as in *The Mutiny Within*, p. 245.

[33] See David Ketterer, *New Worlds for Old: The Apocalyptic Imagination, Science Fiction, and American Literature* (New York: Doubleday Anchor Press; Bloomington: Indiana University Press, 1974), esp. pp. 3-25, 38-39.

[34] *In Search of Frankenstein*, p. 234. For a detailed analysis of Frankenstein's

attempt to wed the transcendent vision of alchemy to the methodology of science, see Irving H. Buchen, *Frankenstein* and the Alchemy of Creation and Evolution," *The Wordsworth Circle*, 8 (Spring, 1977), 103-12.

[35] The tale is included in *Mary Shelley: Collected Tales and Stories*, ed. Charles Robinson (Baltimore: John Hopkins University Press, 1976), pp. 332-44.

[36] See "Mary Shelley and the Roger Dodsworth Hoax," *Keats-Shelley Journal*, 24 (1975), 20-28. The piece is included in *Mary Shelley: Collected Tales and Stories*, pp. 43-50.

[37] On the connection between the literary hoax and science fiction see David Ketterer, "Science Fiction and Allied Literature," *Science-Fiction Studies*, 3 (March, 1976), 70.

[38] The chapel analogy is observed by Small in *Ariel Like a Harpy*, pp. 306-07.

[39] Something of Shelley's immolation seems also to be projected in this description.

[40] Volney's statement is quoted by Florescu in *In Search of Frankenstein*, p. 217.

[41] See, for example, the edition of *Frankenstein* published by the Cornhill Publishing Company of Boston and New York in 1922 and the more recent and widely circulated Signet edition.

[42] "Moral and Myth in Mrs. Shelley's *Frankenstein*," *Keats-Shelley Journal*, 8 (Winter, 1959), 29.

[43] Rieger's 1818 edition, p. 10.

[44] In relating this fact to *Frankenstein*, Rieger quotes a pertinent passage about polar existence from Melville's *Pierre* (1852) : "there, the needle indifferently respects all points of the horizon alike." See *The Mutiny Within*, p. 89; and *Pierre; or, The Ambiguities*, ed. Henry A. Murray (New York: Hendricks House, Inc., 1949), p. 194.

NOTES TO CHAPTER 5

[1] See, in this connection, A. D. Nuttall, *The Common Sky: Philosophy and the Literary Imagination* (London: Chatto and Windus, 1974).

[2] Shelley's *"Prometheus Unbound": A Critical Reading* (Baltimore: The Johns Hopkins Press, 1965), p. 6.

[3] *Ibid.*, p. 4.

[4] *The Letters of Percy Bysshe Shelley*, I, 380.

[5] *The Letters of Edward John Trelawny*, p. 194.

[6] "Frankenstein's Monster and Its Romantic Relatives: Problems of Knowledge in English Romanticism," *Texas Studies in Literature and Language*, 15 (Spring, 1973), 51-65.

[7] *Ibid.*, 57.

[8] *Nature's Work of Art* (New Haven: Yale University Press, 1975).

[9] See, *The Complete Works of Percy Bysshe Shelley*, VII, 60.

[10] See, again in this connection, Milton A. Mays, "*Frankenstein,* Mary Shelley's Black Theodacy."

[11] *Walden,* ed. J. Lyndon Shanley (Princeton, N.J.: Princeton University Press, 1971), p. 306.

[12] *Ariel Like a Harpy,* pp. 215, 293-310; *Billion Year Spree,* p. 23, and *Frankenstein Unbound,* passim; *Mary Shelley's Monster,* pp. 52-65.

[13] *Mary Shelley's Monster,* p. 66.

[14] This distinction between "significance" and "meaning" is elaborated by E. D. Hirsch, Jr., in *Validity in Interpretation* (New Haven: Yale University Press, 1967).

[15] See Tropp's doctoral dissertation "Mary Shelley's Monster: A Study of *Frankenstein*" (Boston University, 1973), p. 26. Tropp's book on *Frankenstein* presents his dissertation in a substantially revised form and does not include this statement.

[16] "Kinship and Guilt in Mary Shelley's *Frankenstein,*" 39.

[17] "Mary Shelley's Modern Prometheus: A Study in the Ethics of Scientific Creativity," *Dalhousie Review,* 52 (Summer, 1972), 212-25.

[18] *An Essay Concerning Human Understanding,* ed. Peter H. Nidditch (Oxford: The Clarendon Press, 1975), p. 182.

[19] "Frankenstein's Monster and Its Romantic Relatives: Problems of Knowledge in English Romanticism," 60-61.

[20] See Ketterer, *New Worlds for Old, passim.*

[21] "Frankenstein's Monster and Its Romantic Relatives: Problems of Knowledge in English Romanticism," 62.

[22] See D. G. James, *The Dream of Prospero* (Oxford: The Clarendon Press, 1967).

[23] *Billion Year Spree,* pp. 38-39, n. 30. See also Hartley S. Spatt, "Mary Shelley's Last Men: The Truth of Dreams," *Studies in the Novel* 7 (Winter, 1975), 526-37.

[24] *The Last Man,* ed. Hugh J. Luke, Jr. (Lincoln: University of Nebraska Press, 1965), p. 146.

[25] See *The Novels of Thomas Love Peacock,* ed. David Garnett (London: Hart Davis, 1948), I, 280.

[26] M. A. Goldberg claims that the theme of estrangement in *Frankenstein* has less to do with Mary's loneliness than with the relationship between happiness and social obligation as preached by Godwin and by Paine's *The*

Rights of Man (1791). I would rather say that the theme of estrangement has as much to do with Mary's loneliness as with the logic of solipsistic philosophy. See "Moral and Myth in Mrs. Shelley's *Frankenstein*," 33-38.

NOTES TO THE APPENDIX

[1] *Mary Shelley's Journal*, p. 79.

[2] Introduction to Rieger's 1818 edition, p. xliv.

[3] For the same passage in Rieger's 1818 edition, see p. 60.

[4] *The Letters of Percy Bysshe Shelley*, I, 565.

[5] Introduction to Rieger's 1818 edition, p. xviii.

[6] See the Acknowledgements to Rieger's 1818 edition, p. v.

[7] Introduction to Rieger's 1818 edition, p. xviii.

[8] In Rieger's 1818 edition, see p. 217.

[9] Introduction to Rieger's 1818 edition, p. xxiii.

[10] *Ibid.*, p. xviii.

[11] Rieger claims that his text "reproduces for the first time in more than a century" the 1818 edition. See the Note on the Text, p. xliii. It should be observed that Rieger is overlooking editions of the 1818 text published in 1932 and 1937. Spurred by Rieger's example, the 1818 text is also reproduced in *The Annotated "Frankenstein,"* ed. Leonard Wolf (New York: Clarkson N. Potter, Inc., 1977). For arguments against the additional reasons that Wolf advances for preferring the original version, see my review-essay, "*Frankenstein* in Wolf's Clothing," *Science-Fiction Studies*, 6 (July, 1979), 216-20.

[12] The Note on the Text of Rieger's 1818 edition, p. xliv.

[13] Rieger's 1818 edition, p. 140.

[14] *Ibid.*, p. 78.